Carolyn   August 1990

m. H.

D0536479

WINNING
WITHOUT DRUGS

This book is dedicated to
Peter and Adrian, Stefan and Julius, Gareth and Owain,
who comprise part of the next generation who
can fulfil their potential naturally.

WINNING WITHOUT DRUGS

The Natural Approach to Competitive Sport

DAVID HEMERY MBE
GUY OGDEN AND ALAN EVANS

WILLOW BOOKS
COLLINS
1990

The authors are grateful to the following, whose views and writings have significantly influenced the genesis of this book: Tim Gallwey, Sir John Whitmore, Alan Fine, Eugene Halliday, Andrew Nash, Mike Harrington, Jeff Galloway.

We wish particularly to thank Toni Griffiths and Jan Dryden for their editorial help, and Rachel Norman, Michelle Southwood and Margaret Pike for typing the manuscript and meeting very tight deadlines.

Willow Books
William Collins Sons & Co Ltd
London · Glasgow · Sydney · Auckland
Toronto · Johannesburg

First published 1990
© David Hemery, Guy Ogden and Alan Evans 1990
Illustrations by Will Giles and Sonia Pond

A CIP catalogue record for this book is available from the British Library

ISBN 0 00 218349 8

Set in Trump Medieval by Ace Filmsetting Ltd, Frome, Somerset
Printed and bound in Great Britain by William Collins Sons & Co Ltd, Glasgow

CONTENTS

INTRODUCTION

This book is an act of defiance. It stems from our firm belief that it is possible to achieve excellence in sport at the highest levels without resorting to unnatural and illegal aids such as steroids and other performance-enhancing drugs that both damage the human body and debase and defile competitive sport.

Dr Roger Bannister, in his book *The Four Minute Mile* (1989), said: 'The aim is to move with the greatest possible freedom towards the realisation of the best that is within us.' It is our strong conviction that practitioners in all forms of competitive sport can, by a fundamental reappraisal of their approach to athletic preparation, significantly improve their performance and realize the best that is within them.

The chapters of this book provide powerful advocacy for natural approaches to body maintenance and training techniques as steps on the path towards realizing an athlete's full potential. The case is comprehensively argued – technically, analytically and philosophically – that limits to human performance can be rolled back by means which are not only wholesome and life-enhancing but which can help to ensure that the unfair and dangerous recourse to drugs will not necessarily lead to triumph in competition.

The book draws upon new knowledge available from both orthodox and non-orthodox sources, an approach which has implications for sportsmen and women as they train for their particular sports performance. A careful consideration of this new knowledge suggests there is a need to reappraise current practice in a number of areas of athletic preparation, including training programmes, mobility and stretching techniques, dietary practices, weight training, footwear design, injury diagnosis, treatment and rehabilitation and the combating of physical and mental obstacles to improved performance.

The book advocates a holistic approach to planning and preparation for competitive sport, an approach thus far neglected by many coaches and performers. The view is firmly put forward that an integrated programme of athletic preparation – encompassing the physical, mental, emotional and ideological aspects of one's regime – will pay dividends in improving performance, diminishing or avoiding injury time and lengthening the span over which sportsmen and women can sustain quality athletic performances at the highest level.

This book is directed to all sportsmen and women, whatever their field, who wish to have greater knowledge and control of their own bodies and their capacities for excellence. It is our hope that the radical approaches advocated will lead to a new sense of empowerment and fulfilment amongst performers who choose to adopt and adapt these approaches in their own striving for excellence.

David Hemery MBE
Guy Ogden
Alan Evans

1

THE MIND
IS
THE KEY

David Hemery

The key factor which separates the human who achieves his potential from the one who does not is the use of the mind.

Here is why:

● Even if you have the greatest amount of talent imaginable, what do you still have to do in order to fulfil your potential? What can you not avoid? The answer . . . practice or hard work.

● And do you think you will actually do the necessary hard work or practice if you have low commitment? . . . Very doubtful.

● And do you think you'll make that commitment and stay with the task unless you have enthusiasm? . . . Probably not.

So what is it that you can become enthusiastic about? The answer to that is a clear aim or goal, which is a positive, challenging and attainable vision. Vision, as used here, refers to the creative use of your imagination. It's under your mental control and it's the starting point of the achievement process. Expanded potential for yourself begins with your creative thought. Your use of your mind is the starting point on the road to fulfilling potential, the bridge between ambition and achievement.

It is a breathtaking realization that, given the parameters of each individual's capabilities, the size of your achievement is limited only by the size of your initial vision. You control your future achievements through your thoughts. If your goal is challenging and attainable, your vision clear, your enthusiasm and commitment full on the task, then little can stop you achieving your aim.

Reviewing these factors, the starting point is establishing clarity for each goal. What do you want to achieve? Answer this question first, then progress through the other elements. Each aspect needs to be positive and aligned in order to optimize personal performance.

THOUGHT	*clarity of goal*
	positive vision
	challenging and attainable goal
FEELING	*enthusiasm*
	like/dislike
WILL	*intention*
	commitment
ACTION	*practice*
	performance

If you are truly interested in achieving your aims you need to discover how much you have invested in each of these aspects. You do this by assessing your investment on a 1-10 scale (with 10 high) and by facing the following questions:

● What do I need to know and do in order to achieve my aim, step by step?
● How enthusiastic am I about the aim and each necessary step? How could I raise any low enthusiasm? e.g. by making a disliked step a challenge.
● What level of commitment do I have to the aim and to each individual step?

Scoring each segment will give you a clear indication as to

how positive you are and how personally aligned in fulfilling your aim.

GOAL-SETTING

The goal you set may be a long-term ambition or it may be a single part of one practice session on the way to a short-term or long-term aim; whatever the case, the principles remain the same. The goal, and each intermediate step, should be agreed upon by you and your coach, and there should be honest assessment of performance throughout the programme. The goal should be challenging, yet attainable, so that both hope and motivation are maintained. There must be a clear, positive vision of the goal. Improvement should be measurable and geared to producing the best performance at the right time. The coach and the athlete should be aware of their individual and joint responsibilities. These ingredients of clearly defined goal-setting are examined in more depth in the remainder of this chapter.

CLARITY OF GOAL

The first, the most important, and probably the most difficult of the stages is establishing clarity of your goal. Long-term goals need regular review for their continuing appropriateness; however, even at the beginning when attempting to become clear about the direction and requirements of a goal, reviewing is an important part of the process. Often what may appear to be your goal at the start of discussion may well turn out to be only a symptom of a different goal. For example, your goal might be to learn how to dance. In clarifying that goal, you discover that the desired skill is only a tool for a different goal, which might be to have access to a wider social circle. Recognition of the different objective may allow you to choose another route. Throughout the year it will be necessary to reassess and restate your goals and the steps to achieving the long-term aims.

A REALISTIC AND CHALLENGING GOAL

If your long-term sport aim has been set too high, it's possible to feel overwhelmed with the impossibility of the task. The extreme case of someone setting his sights too high is the perfectionist, who is doomed to failure. Also, even if the goal is realistic, circumstances often change – injury or sickness, a job move or a personal life trauma may make the original aim impossible to achieve. If your goal is not modified in these situations then you can rapidly become demotivated and want to quit.

At the other extreme, if your goal is set too low, you will also lack motivation. Where there is no challenge and the task is too easy you will not feel motivated to start. If you do start, the chances are high that you will soon lose interest and again feel like stopping the activity.

Research has shown that setting challenging and attainable goals is in itself motivating. One big question is: what do each of us see as a challenging and attainable level?

A fine illustration of a performer who made a long-term, highly challenging goal attainable is John Naber. As a university student in California, he watched Mark Spitz win his multiple gold medals in the 1972 Olympics. John resolved that he would win the 100 metres backstroke in the next Games in Montreal. He knew that in order to be in with a realistic chance of achieving that goal he would have to aim to break the world record; and in order to do that he would have to take five seconds off his personal best time. In 100 metres that's a sizeable chunk of time.

In order to make his goal attainable, he divided the five seconds by the number of hours he had available to train in the intervening four years. He worked out that he would have to improve by only one twelve hundredth of a second for every hour he spent training. And that he equated to approximately one fifth of an eye blink. He thought to himself, well if I work intelligently as well as hard I'm sure I can improve by one fifth of an eye blink for every hour I spend training. His progress was so good that he was chosen to captain the US swimming team in 1976. He won the 100 metres backstroke in a new world record, and the 200 metres in an Olympic record. The process obviously worked!

This example demonstrates a basic principle concerning the setting of long term goals, namely the importance of breaking them down into attainable steps. Each step should be within an achievable time scale or framework, and the steps should be under constant review in order to, if necessary, re-establish the goals.

All too often unnecessary limits are *self-imposed*. I once spent an evening with a group of twenty schoolboys, aged twelve to seventeen, who had been specially selected by the LTA as Britain's brightest tennis prospects. Towards the end of the evening with them I asked if they could imagine holding up the cup at Wimbledon. Could they imagine what that would be like, smiling to the crowd as they turned to show the trophy? After a few seconds a couple of the boys shook their heads saying that they just couldn't imagine that. I pointed out that if they weren't in the ball park physically they wouldn't have been chosen to be at the National Centre. If a performer limits his imagination then he limits his options. Obviously, not everyone can win Wimbledon, but why rule out the possibility and impose a self-limitation – at least ten years ahead of time?

Dr Christiaan Barnard, the first human heart transplant surgeon, said he believed that man could achieve anything within the scope of his imagination. If you can't clearly imagine yourself doing the next step in your athletic progression, then there is much less chance of your making progress.

Fear of failure can cause you to lower the challenge you set for yourself. Lowering your challenge may ensure against your failing but it will also inhibit your potential. Anxious and negative thought will not help performance. What can you do about them? Recognition of what you're doing to yourself is the first step. You have to become aware of when your thoughts start to increase your anxiety. Then see if there is a positive opposite which could be your new focus. For example, if your anxious thoughts are creating a feeling of listlessness, imagine the opposite of listlessness and adopt that posture in mind and body; it might be alertness or readiness.

POSITIVE AND NEGATIVE
VISION

The goal must be stated in the positive. Why? What happens if you are told, 'Don't think of a red balloon'? If you have any imagination your mind will be filled with a vision of the very thing you have been ordered not to think of. Bringing that into a sport context, a typical negative instruction might be, 'Don't get out first ball!' It is intended to help but will probably create only increased tension.

It is interesting to note that top level performers are usually very good at mentally visualizing experiences. If the thought is negative the image which is filling the brain tends to draw unwanted action from the performer. Every mental image tends to objectify only itself. In other words, your actions follow your thoughts. If that is true then filling your thoughts with positive goals will create a greater likelihood of positive outcomes.

If you are interested in positive results then you must be aware of negative thoughts creeping in. Worrying about what the opposition might do is not constructive thought. Awareness of what the opposition might do and thoughts of what would be your best response is positive and constructive. Catch the onset of negative thought and replace it with a positive opposite.

Our creative thought is our greatest gift; however, it may be used positively or negatively. I have two very personal illustrations of this. First the positive example:

In the weeks prior to the 400 metres hurdles in the 1968 Mexico City Olympics I rehearsed every option I could imagine, thinking through how I could do my best in each situation: e.g. drawn on an inside lane, where I could see all my opponents, I imagined myself remaining focused on my lane with my ideal pace even though I could imagine someone else racing off at breakneck pace. I rehearsed the same sort of control and judgement drawn in lane eight and running blind all the way, retaining confidence to execute world record attempting pace. Through weather changes – head wind, tail wind, rain or heat – all options were run with the leg speed and stride length to bring me through the race with as close to an ideal time for me as I could imagine.

The heat and the semi-final were also raced, mentally, at a predetermined level of effort and pace which I hoped would be sufficient to qualify me. Included in my planning was the flexibility of changed pace and awareness of others which I hoped would ensure I advanced to the final.

Each segment was thought through and sensed with such detail that my pulse rate and breathing would be close to matching the physical sensations of the race. This was done as I was lying on my bunk bed or after supper, walking around a different lane of the practice track imagining the precise pace, effort distribution, foot placements and hurdling motion to lead me to doing the best I thought was possible at that time.

The pattern worked ideally. Each race was executed as planned, with the exception that the last half of the final was run even faster than I had thought. Perhaps that was from added adrenalin flow or the assistance of less air resistance at 7500 feet. Whatever it was, the result was as positive as I could have hoped for; almost a second taken off the world record and an Olympic gold, in one.

The second personal example was my use of negative thought. Prior to the 1972 Munich Olympics I thought that it was important to face the possibility of losing. I would be four years older and there could be faster, younger, stronger opponents. Certainly that was a real possibility. My best response would have been to have acknowledged that as a possible outcome and also to have recognised that I could not control how well others were going to perform. The only control I could have was over how well I could run. Instead, I thought that it would be mature to face losing and come to terms with my feelings if that happened. Could I live with being a loser?

I thereby allowed my thoughts to review negative images of myself in two ways. First, I repeatedly visualized myself losing Olympic races. Second, I was labelling everything but winning as being losing. More on the second point later.

I spent two months anguishing over different images of myself losing races. I didn't like the feelings associated with losing but I finally became numb, not feeling anything, repeatedly saying to myself, 'It's okay, you're just going to try your hardest to do your best!' The result of this self-hypnosis was that on the day of the 400 metres hurdles final I woke up totally emotionless – without enthusiasm or nerves. By the time I had warmed up and was entering the stadium I was digging my nails into my hands, saying to myself, 'For goodness sake wake up: this is the Olympic final', and the programmed voice came back, 'Yes, and you're just going to try your hardest to do your best.'

I had no clear vision of *how* I would run the final. I had read the inspirational book *Jonathan Livingston Seagull* by Richard Bach, and believed that there were no limits; I would just go out and run a limitless race. I went out and tried to run with a hundred per cent effort all the way. Race effort distribution is very subtle and I was running with low awareness and a lot of effort. Ideally there should be high awareness and only appropriately channelled effort. I realized that all was not well with a 100 metres to go and I felt my legs weakening. My mind and will forced me to the line and I finished third, only two inches out of the silver but nowhere near my potential from my year's work. There were other mitigating circumstances, such as a slight thigh muscle pull three weeks before the Games, but I believe that far more than any physical hold back, my mental approach was at fault. I wasn't in tune in body, mind and spirit. My thoughts were not clear, my enthusiasm was nowhere near what was needed and I was left willing my body through the effort. One out of three will not produce the best results of which we are capable. The point of this story is that it provides an illustration of how negative thought and negative imaging can restrict potential and deny a positive outcome. Negative mental images are powerful and unhelpful.

Returning to the point of labelling non-first-place finishers as losers, I believe strongly in the perspective of Britain's National Coaching Foundation who advocate having two distinct goals – performance improvement goals and end goals. They are written here in the correct order, because the performer has significant control over the first and much less over the second. Winning, making the team, getting the cup are all end goals. If performers are in with a chance, I believe that they should be aiming for those but they must be the second goal. The way to get there is by the first goal – performance improvement. I was aiming to win the 1968 Olympics. My route to that was to train physically and mentally towards a performance improvement which would put me in with the best possible chance of achieving it.

By valuing only winning (an end goal), a superb performance by two individuals in a race only allows praise for one. One wins, the other loses. Having performance improvement as the first goal provides everyone with a way of additionally congratulating the performer who doesn't win the title but has set a personal best.

RIGHT TIME, RIGHT PLACE

The next aspect of the goal-setting process is that your personal best should be achieved when you want it most. It's of little use to you competitively if you only improve in training. The context will change according to the steps on the way to your long term goal. You may, for example, need to establish a first-rate performance in a qualifying competition and then to produce an even better performance, days or weeks later, in a championship event.

MEASURABLE IMPROVEMENT

Another goal factor is that, ideally, each goal step should be quantifiable. If you set a vague goal, such as wanting to get 'better' at your sport, although it is positive, it is not a clearly defined challenge. In athletics, improving your marathon time by one second is 'better' but that, also, may not be the sort of goal achievement that you would want.

Measurement is easy in sports where higher, further, faster are the criteria. It is less easy in a team sport or where judgements are made on the quality of execution. This provides a challenge for the coach and performer to find ways of determining performance improvement. One such option in team sports is to establish a performance improvement such as the percentage of accurate passes or percentage of shots on goal.

In order to have a quantifiable goal it may be necessary to make a subjective assessment of the quality of an action. For example, in practice you may feel awkward or inhibited performing a particular action. You then define the quality which is the positive opposite, e.g. smooth, flowing, powerful, etc. You rate yourself, on a 1-10 scale, on how smooth, flowing or powerful you feel at the start of the session; then set a challenging but realistic improved score to be reached by the end of the session. You thereby make a measurable goal for the session based on your own sensations. You taught yourself how to walk, ride a bike, and catch a ball by paying attention to what was happening. There is no reason why you can't use your awareness of senses to assist your learning now.

Using this tool to improve personal performance requires a high degree of personal awareness during your training and performance. There is a requirement for accuracy in your perception of what is happening while you are moving. Sharing responsibility for what you learn during training actually prepares you better for competition, where you must be totally self-reliant.

ATTRIBUTION ACCURACY

It will be useful to discuss with your coach what each of you discovered in your performance in training or competition. What were your strengths and where were your weaknesses? Was the aim achieved completely, in part, or not at all? Sometimes your assessment of your play may be coloured by such things as scoring a goal. You might assess that that made the game performance a success, whereas the rest of your play might have been below par. Conversely, if you made one costly mistake which led to a goal being scored against your team, you might allow that negatively to colour your assessment of a generally excellent game performance. For improved performance it will be valuable to look at an accurate assessment of where each problem lies. In a session in which a personal lack of effort might be the real reason for your poor performance, you might have attributed it to bad luck. Equally, it is not helpful to blame yourself for a poor performance which is caused by circumstances beyond your control. This aspect of performance appraisal is referred to as attribution accuracy.

SHARED AND INDIVIDUAL RESPONSIBILITY

If you are working in partnership with a coach or advisor, for best results you will both need to share your goals. If the aspirations of either one of you are higher than the other and this is not explored and agreement reached, there is every likelihood of a major problem. If, for example, you have ambitions to reach national level and your coach doesn't have the time, interest or ability to agree with that aim then, at the very least, frustration ensues. Or if your coach holds secret hopes that you will push yourself to new heights and he hasn't shared these hopes with you, and your primary interest is in the social side of sport contact, then disappointment and frustration are inevitable. In essence, openness and honesty must be built into the goal-setting conversation.

Taking personal responsibility for your positive vision is one of the most vital parts of your armoury as a performer. It can be much easier just to follow instructions, and yet, as mentioned above, you have to take total responsibility when you are performing. Sharing and taking responsibility with a coach or parent in the training stage is a valuable learning step and a preparation tool. It provides a step towards greater maturity through personal development. It is probably the hardest step for you or any athlete to take. The coach is usually older, more experienced and 'expected' to know the 'right' things for you to do. To an extent that is true; on the other hand, you will know best what is happening within yourself, if your awareness is adequately developed. Each of us is slightly different in mind, emotions, body and spirit and your input is needed. Unless at some point you are willing to share and take responsibility for your direction and efforts, then you will never fully develop your potential.

Early in life you had to take full responsibility for learning how to walk and run. It was largely an unconscious process but no doubt you were paying a lot of attention to what was happening. Later, when you learned how to ride a bike it was perhaps more conscious but ultimately you had to take responsiblity to peddle off and go for it. Once you had accepted full responsibility for your performance, from then on you owned the experience and the ability to ride.

It may prove just as difficult for your coach to withdraw from total control of you, the performer. Evolution is a vital ingredient of any coach-athlete relationship. Obviously the novice is much more dependent on the coach than an experienced performer. It is important for a coach to recognize that as you develop and increase in awareness you will be able to provide as much, if not more, input than the coach in establishing a challenging goal. It is a shared responsibility.

A coach can often assist as a catalyst, challenging you to greater heights. However, a fine balance is needed between encouragement and pushing. The coach's role is one of an awareness raiser, asking the question: 'What can you achieve?'. For the aspiring athlete there is the question of moral responsibility, how to achieve success without cheating. As we stated in the introduction, we believe sportsmen and women have a responsibility to their higher selves, to achieve to the best of their abilities.

TIME-PHASED IMPROVEMENT

Once a goal has been clarified it is helpful to determine the steps in a logical, time-sequenced progression.

Billy Smith, my coach while I was at university, provided a useful reminder of where my focus needed to be. We had set our long-term goal to break the world record in the Olympics in October 1968. During March I had time-phased my improvement by writing half a second improvement beside every month. I felt quite put off when Billy leant over and crossed out all the months beyond the first three. However, his words explained: 'Easter is no time to be getting excited about Christmas!' The old north country adage is apt – 'Inch by inch, it's a cinch, yard by yard, it's bloody hard!' And you only take one step at a time. I understood the message – focus on what you can get to grips with. Focus on the now; after all, that is the only time in which we can actually operate.

─────── *SUMMARY* ───────
Improving performance through goal-setting and visualization

- Set a goal which is achievable yet challenging.

- Your vision of the goal should be both clear and positive.

- Come to an understanding with your coach on responsibilities and ultimate goals.

- Improvement should be measurable, time-phased and geared to producing the optimum performance at the right time.

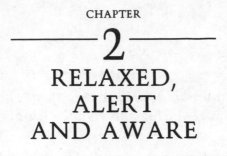

2
RELAXED, ALERT AND AWARE

David Hemery

Your state of mind directly affects how you perform. Your body responds to your thoughts. If you are really angry you may clench your teeth and tighten your fists. If you are apprehensive, tension will be represented somewhere in your body – perhaps your stomach, shoulders or neck. When you are asleep your body is usually completely relaxed. If you are aiming for peak performance you want to be in a state of readiness; mentally and physically you want to be neither too tense nor too relaxed. Often performers waste energy by holding unnecessary muscle tension. Your body does not wish to hold such tension and will release it if the mind is alerted to it. An example of this is when someone who has been driving against the clock is asked how tense his neck and shoulders are. The mind focusses on the area, becomes aware of the tension, and the inhibiting muscles relax.

Mentally the ideal is to be appropriately aware, alert and relaxed. What can you do which will enable you to be in this state? How can you remain relaxed with the build-up of apprehension and anxiety before competition? What will assist your state of mind so that you will be in peak readiness?

RELAXATION

Through appropriate physical relaxation and positive imagery you can release the tension which saps energy and inhibits performance. Achieving a state of physical and mental readiness, at will, is a learnable skill. Taking the first of these two, how can you use your mind to relax physically?

There are many variations of muscle relaxation. If you have several hours before a competition, the extreme option is sleep. Some performers, including Seb Coe and myself, have catnapped on the day of a major competition. This is one of the mind/body's constructive ways of avoiding tension and worrying thought. You may not find daytime sleep helpful if you awaken feeling groggy and therefore have difficulty preparing yourself mentally. The only way of finding out whether it could be helpful for you is to try it.

In the wakeful state, your mind can be used to focus attention on progressive relaxation. One method of increasing your awareness of your body and how to relax it, is to contract specific parts of your body for about five seconds. At the same time you may hold your breath. You breathe out as you release the contracted muscle group. You may find that you need to repeat some areas to feel them fully relax. You progress through the whole body, starting from your feet and working up to your head.

BREATHING

Using your breath as a tool of relaxation is extremely valuable. Your rate and depth of breathing can be used consciously to modify your heart rate, muscular and mental tension, blood pressure, etc. Various machines can be used to give you a measurement of this in a process known as 'biofeedback'.

These machines can provide helpful statistical verification of the internal alterations you are achieving through your actions and thoughts.

If you are anxious and breathing rapidly and shallowly, deepen and slow down your breathing rate in order to relax. The result of rapid breathing caused by anxiety will be to upset your oxygen and carbon dioxide balance. The resulting light-headedness will leave you in a state less capable of appropriate relaxation, alertness and awareness. Taking longer, slower breaths will help you to regain necessary mental focus and balance.

Simply observing your breathing is a tool of meditation which allows your thoughts to be in the present rather than worrying about past or future events. Mentally saying, 'breathe in' on the intake and 'breathe out' on the output will give your mind something to focus on. You may assist your focus on this task by observing how accurately you can sense the exact transition to each phase.

PERFORMANCE RELAXATION

When you are told to relax during performance, you may not know how to go about it. Some assume that relaxing means having the muscles lose all their tension. That may be as unhelpful as too much tension, particularly just prior to and during a competitive performance. One athlete discovered that on hearing the word 'relax' during a race, he would drop effort and slow down. He found the substitute words, 'faster, looser' much more useful. Different words will create different images and effects in each individual. With this in mind it is well worth discovering which are the best trigger words for yourself.

AWARENESS

MENTAL TRAINING AND INCREASED AWARENESS DURING ACTIVITY

Many performers are loath to sacrifice much active training time for purely mental work. The recommendation here is that you begin to develop mental skills and learn how to focus attention *during* active sessions. Obviously some mental training sessions will require a quiet place to relax and practise these skills. However, several approaches may be experimented with during physical practice time, such as:

● Retaining the intention/purpose of your training session in your conscious mind during its execution should enhance its effectiveness.

● Setting up a competition in practice so that any adverse reactions are experienced and coping with strategies may be developed. During this practice competition, apart from the physical experiences, pay attention to any negative thoughts which arise. What prompted them? What options do you have for positive thoughts? See if you can notice any difference in tension and performance if you replace a negative thought with a positive one. This approach of simulation is known as 'desensitizing training'.

● Focusing your attention on the process of execution will enable your body to perform with greater fluidity. On the basis that the body does not naturally want to hold tension, discovering it allows it to release itself. We need to rediscover the level of experiencing we had when we taught ourselves how to walk, talk, catch a ball and ride a bike. These were primarily achieved through discovery. This level of self-aware observation of experience can be used to continually enhance your performance.

Expanding on this last point, mental focus may be used to raise your awareness of the current state of any specific part of your body. Again progressing from your toes to your head, you may consciously focus your attention on the pressure, heat, contact points, tension levels, etc., in each area. While performing in training, your aim is to become more conscious of your sensory experience. You will soon be able to identify areas which feel awkward and need modification and other aspects which feel great.

BECOMING FOCUSED
ON THE PROCESS

Heightened awareness of what is going on, either within yourself or in your competitive situation, can be a useful tool to enhance performance. Another amazing function of staying focused on the process, as it is happening, is that there is no tension in each successive instant. Unfortunately staying in the *now* is practically impossible. Most of us recognize that this is not a new problem. It is reported that some 2500 years ago Plato likened the mind to a ship whose crew had mutinied. The captain and the navigator have been locked up below and the crew members, whom he likened to our thoughts, are taking it in turns to steer. One will steer for a while, then get bored and wander off, and another will take his place and steer in a new direction.

There is a way of returning the captain and navigator to their rightful positions to assist us in focusing our attention appropriately. This is done by self-questioning. The captain knows where you want to go. The whole area of goal-setting is concerned with one question, 'Where do you want to go?' In performance terms that is, 'What do you want to achieve?' Four-time Olympic discus champion, Al Oerter, believes that 'targeting' is our most vital mental focus. Our next question is one of awareness. 'Where are we now?' Knowing exactly where we are at every instant is the role of the navigator in us, and monitoring that at every instant is what is meant by staying focused on the now. What exactly are you experiencing at every moment?

Awareness of what you are experiencing at every instant is your route to relaxed concentration and effective performance. In reality, *the only time we have is now.* Our thoughts may focus on past, present or future, each of which, at times, can provide useful perspectives, but the only time in which we can *do anything* is the present. So if you are interested in improving your performance then the place to focus your primary attention during training and competition is in the immediate present.

SINGLE FOCUS

Single mindedness has often been cited as a contributing factor to success. However, single mindedness as a way of moving towards an ultimate achievement may move you out of balance in your social setting. The result may be a distancing from partner, coach or work mates. There need not be anything so serious as a split in a partnership, but there will be a need for understanding.

Several athletes have shared with me that they felt in complete harmony in themselves – body, mind and spirit – but on the social level things were not as good. My own experience, particularly during periods of preparation for the Olympics, was that there was a chosen time of detachment from social life so that focus could be total on the upcoming personal challenge. Conversations and relationships were still friendly, but the main focus of attention was on the event.

Top athletes are generally well integrated internally. Their inner harmony, coupled with an intensity of intention, will achieve, for them, the highest levels of success.

Vital for athletes in any sport must be to ensure that the focus of attention is appropriate. Performance focus, with enthusiasm and total commitment, will result in achievement of any imaginable aim.

If you can get yourself into this state of body, mind and spirit integration, I believe that achievement beyond drugs is possible. Drugs may manipulate your body into states which can be achieved through the mind. However, you could become a passenger on a train that you don't control. It's your mind, your self-belief and self-confidence which can, step by step, take you to any target you wish to set for yourself which is within the range of possibility.

A HELPFUL FOCUS
DURING DISCOMFORT

Using marathons as an illustration, some runners use distraction techniques to avoid physical discomfort. They attempt to ignore it by looking around, placing their attention on the scenery or a mental image but most of the top performers have their full attention on their own process.

If some of your training or competition involves 'hanging on while hurting', here is a tool worth trying. It is a method of monitoring your process of discomfort. As a performer you may be running a set distance at a challenging pace. At some time during this run your mind will bring forward the message, 'Slow down!'. Usually that idea pops into the mind long before your body needs to slow down. If the intention of your training or competitive run is to make a hard effort, the following is a sequence of self-questioning you can go through:

what is it that has led to this thought? Check out which part of your body is least comfortable. Suppose it's the diaphragm, which has been heaving with the effort, resulting in a genuine feeling of discomfort and perhaps a slight feeling of sickness. The question you then ask yourself is: 'How would I rate this discomfort on a 1–10 scale?' – with 10 putting me in hospital and 0 being no discomfort at all. For the sake of illustration, suppose your rating was 6 or 7. The next question would be: 'What number would it have to be on to make me stop?' Suppose your answer to that was 9. Then for the remainder of your run monitor the gradual increase towards that 9; 7.1, 7.2, etc. The chances are very good that your discomfort rating will not get above about 7.8 before your session is completed.

——— *SUMMARY* ———
Relaxed, alert and aware

- **Muscle relaxation and controlled breathing can be learned.**

- **Practise mental training whilst engaged in physical activity.**

- **Concentrate on the *now*.**

- **When nearing major competition, avoid unnecessary distractions.**

- **Overcome physical discomfort by rating it.**

3

VISUALIZATION AND MENTAL TRAINING

David Hemery

In my study of sports highest achievers, (*The Pursuit of Sporting Excellence*, Collins, 1986) I personally interviewed 63 individuals. Each in their sport, in their era, was the best in the world. Some said that they were not aware of having used imagery of mental rehearsal; however, 80 per cent said that they had and that they found it invaluable! They had just done it intuitively and it is now apparent that high achievers in every field of endeavour have done the same. It has only been in recent years that the practice has been identified and words used to describe it. Now all those who are interested in developing and fulfilling their potential have come to recognize that if they have the capacity to imagine, they too can use visualization to assist their performance.

The sort of visualization or mental images you should create depends on the intention of your action. As used here, imagery and mental rehearsal are distinguished as follows: positive imagery is using your imagination in *preparation for* good performance, positive mental rehearsal is using your imagination to *preview* the best you could imagine doing in the upcoming performance.

Imagery

You can use your imagination to enhance your performance at any time and anywhere. Several uses will be reflected below, beginning with the most calming.

Calmness
and Anxiety Control

For best results in the beginning it will be helpful to start in a calm environment. With practice you will probably find it less necessary to have a physically calm environment. However, to begin with, find yourself a location where you feel comfortable and unstressed and can *mentally* relax. A somewhat darkened room will cut down visual stimulus; cotton wool in the ears will cut down noise distractions. You should sit or lie in a position which will allow for relaxation, without prompting sleep. Have your head and lower back supported and close your eyes.

If your intention is to learn to calm yourself in an anxiety-producing time prior to competition, imagine yourself in a situation where you are able to let go of unnecessary tension. Provide yourself, in your imagination, with a familiar, positive and controllable environment. This may be an imagined or real location and will vary with each performer. Typical places are a lake side; woods; a beach; a quiet room; a mountain side. In fact a suitable place is anywhere you feel free and detached from the excessive pressure that is felt in a competitive environment.

The most simple starting point is to establish a visual image. The majority of our stimulus awareness is dominated by our vision. As you gain the sense that you can see yourself in that location, the most valuable progression is to experience the situation from inside. Initially, with eyes closed, you imagine what it would look like if you were actually there.

The next progression is to add other senses. The more vividly you can experience yourself in the situation, the greater the effect the image will have. Imagine the location in the fullest possible sensory detail; experience the sights, sounds, smells, feelings and even the tastes of the area. Notice your thoughts and emotional feelings.

The intention is to experience safety, familiarity, happiness, contentment or relaxation in this chosen environment. You may choose to stay and experience that quiet place for five or ten minutes and come back relaxed and unstressed. In this place your mind can find a calm state, instead of dwelling on negative, unproductive thoughts.

Mental exercises such as this are now referred to as mental training. The use of the word training implies that there is a need for practice. If it is reasonable to assume that the mind does play a major part in how well you perform, then is it not worth scheduling practice time to assist you to move closer to fulfilling your potential? How much time should be spent in off-the-field practice will depend on each performer.

When you are learning a new skill, be it physical or mental, greater practice time is needed than when refining or maintaining that skill. It may prove useful in an initial stage to be guided through various mental areas by listening to the audio tapes specifically made for performers.[*]

IMAGES FOR
PRE-COMPETITION READINESS

For many performers there is a time lasting from minutes to

[*] Details from The National Coaching Foundation, 4 College Close, Beckett Park, Leeds, LS6 3QH. 0532-744802.

days before a major competition when their thoughts create anxiety within themselves. Thoughts which lead you towards panic will certainly not help your performance. Imagery can be used to control the pre-competition state of mind. The object of this is to focus your thoughts on aspects which will be helpful and minimize time spent worrying about aspects which are unhelpful and/or outside your control.

Prior to competition you need to feel physically and mentally ready. One key mental element is the self-confidence to do your best in the current circumstances. An image which can help to increase your confidence is to relive mentally a previous successful performance. How did it feel? What was your confident body posture? Where was your attention? Again the idea is to experience the feeling of being there and carrying that confidence into your new encounter.

You may find that familiarity with the competitive environment will assist your feeling of confidence. Most people hold some fear of the unknown, so visiting an unfamiliar or new competitive venue before you have to compete there can take away some of the unknowns. It will also give you a clearer context in which to prepare your mental rehearsal.

Tennis star John Newcombe made friends with the environment in which he had to compete. Once the stadium was empty, the day before he was due to play on Centre Court at Wimbledon, he would go to the top of the stands. As he looked down, he extended his arms mentally to embrace the whole court imagining it as a close friend. He wanted to create a sense that he would be comfortable and at home in the place in which he would have to compete the next day.

An interesting use of imagery was employed by Jackie Stewart prior to his Grand Prix races. The day before the race he had a sense of himself as an over-inflated beach ball, bouncing off walls and pavements out of control. He gradually let the air out of this ball, deflating it, so that it was sufficiently under control to bounce between his hand and the pavement. By the time he entered his car at the start of the race he was emotionless. He would not have reacted to a wise-crack or a joke. Jackie had projected his anxiety onto an outside object, in this case a ball, and reduced it in size through his imagination. He thereby gained control of that part of himself.

At times your mind may try to over-control the actions of your body and actually inhibit your potential. One way of breaking this is to imagine a better performer whom you admire. You first imagine visually their action. The next stage is to imagine how it would feel to be that person. Then, as long as it's safe, you just do the action as if you were that better performer. Quite often the body executes a great approximation, based on the improved mental picture being held in the mind.

Intense exercise stresses and to some extent breaks down your body. The recovery period is the time in which your body rebuilds itself. Imagery may be used during your recovery time to rebuild your body, including the results you want from that training session. If you are aiming to enhance your shape, size, strength, speed, stamina or flexibility, hold an impression of your single most desired end result. This may be done between repetitions or at the end of your practice. The more vivid and detailed your imagination the greater will be the benefit. Arnold Schwarzenegger, the body builder, believes that this image of his aim was a major contributory factor for him in reshaping his body.

The term 'active imagery' is used to denote the process whereby the mind creates an image while the body is moving. During the warm-up for my Olympic 400 metres hurdle semi-final in 1968, I saw the American co-favourite, Geoff Vanderstock, take a practice start. My focus of attention left my warm-up and went onto how awesome his speed looked. I felt my heart hit my throat and I instantly recognized the feeling as a first stage of potentially unhelpful fear.

There are two points here. First, I had to be aware that my response to what I saw was potentially unhelpful, i.e. shock thoughts and a constricted feeling in the throat. Secondly, I had to recognize that there was nothing I could do about how fast he ran. I had to find a way of coming back into a state of relaxed concentration and appropriate focus on something which was positive and under my control.

I responded by immediately revisiting, mentally, a place where I had felt exhilarated, fit and strong. The infield grass at the warm-up area was damp from the afternoon rain. With bare feet I strode down the infield. My mental experience was remembering running with speed and flow for hundreds of yards along a firm beach, in six inches of water. I felt the sun on my back and the fullness of my health, strength and power, with no tiring. I did not press my pace; I just relived the sensations and instead of shortness of breath and anxiety, my thoughts were filled with these positive images and sensations. My breathing became deeper and slower. Within seconds I had become absorbed in the good feeling of energy running through me. I was back under control after vividly reliving a relevant positive experience.

SIMULATING
CHALLENGE DURING TRAINING

Many runners have spoken of their use of imagination during solo training. The use is primarily to create the stimulus to enhance performance effort. At the point when your body is beginning to send the message, 'Let's slow down', the imagination can be used to call a challenging foe to your shoulder. That creates a stimulus to maintain pace and keep ahead of this imagined person, who is half a stride behind. It is another method of aligning your thought, feeling and will to enhance your performance.

Irish hammer champion Pat O'Callaghan imagined competitors, while training alone, by setting flags on the field where their hammers had landed. Before leaving the practice field he would have beaten every mark. When he felt under pressure in an international competition, he mentally revisited his training field and said to himself, 'I just have to beat the flags.'

Mental images which stimulate you may be helpful during training; however, the opposite is usually required before major competitions. If you feel very keyed up you will need to steady and calm yourself.

MENTAL REHEARSAL

Consciously or unconsciously, your body executes what your mind thinks. Mental rehearsal provides you with the opportunity to imagine and therefore create your future performance. Your rehearsal must be focused on what you can successfully execute. You imagine yourself in the forthcoming competition.

Jackie Stewart wanted to perform optimally from the start line. While he sat waiting on the starting grid, he imagined the race track coming towards him at 180 mph. As soon as the flag dropped he was into the race and immediately establishing dominance.

Five minutes prior to going out onto the pitch for a rugby international, Willie John McBride, as captain, would tell his players, 'Go and make peace with yourselves.' The players were being asked to centre themselves, eliminate the distractions and centre on what they could control – themselves. At the close of that time, Carwyn James, their coach, would then say, 'Now go out there and express yourselves.' Instruction was not expressed in the negative, such as, 'Don't hold back'. They were given the freedom to be fully themselves, to express all that they were capable of as rugby players.

Some eastern block throwers claim to have spent 70 per cent of their time training physically and 30 per cent training mentally, particularly in the early stages of their careers. As their experience increases so the emphasis shifts. Towards the end of his career, the great Soviet hammer thrower, Yuri Sedek, claimed to be spending only 40 per cent of his training in physical endeavour and 60 per cent in mental training.

Many coaches in both East and West have come to recognize that training physically at no more than 80 per cent of maximum effort is far more conducive to long-term health and improvement than is breaking down from over-intensive training. If top effort performance is limited in training, the use of mental rehearsal, imagining the faster or more precise performance, is not only sound but essential.

It is well worth checking whether you are leaving your best efforts on the practice track or in the warm-up arena. Is there any point in trying to prove to the opposition how good you are then if you do no better, or even a bit worse, in the competition? The best efforts must be saved for when it really counts.

APPROPRIATE FOCUS

The appropriateness of your mental focus is vital. At various times you may need broad or narrow visual and mental focus. The most important aspect to discover is what will be the most helpful focus. This brings us back to the emphasis of the first two chapters. Clarity of goal-setting is the first and most vital stage. An illustration of this was my trying to imagine every possible variable in mentally rehearsing my Olympic races in Mexico.

The aim is for you to use your imagination to experience yourself performing your goal, i.e. doing the best you can imagine you could – a goal that is both challenging and attainable. It will be of most value if you can sense it, so that it feels as though you've been through it. Imagine how you would best handle yourself to stay calm and focused no matter what might happen. Throw in a lot of 'What ifs' – such factors as delays, extra trials, weather changes, schedule changes, competitive arena changes, time interruptions, and hassle from anyone – competitor, coach, referee/umpire, official, administrator, security, spectators, etc. Ask yourself, 'What would be the best performance of which I'm capable?'

It is important to experience exceptionally good conditions and unusual advantage as well as adversity. If you have anticipated achieving a challenging and realistic progression to a certain level in a tournament and for some reason you progress further, you need to be prepared to maintain your concentration, enthusiasm and intention to fulfil potential on this next level as well. It may take a great deal of practice and self-discipline to go through this process. And just as with physical conditioning, the more you mentally practise the more capable you will become and the greater will be the benefits. A couple of obvious benefits are as follows:

● You can mentally rehearse the next step in an activity which you have not yet attempted physically. It is possible for you to imagine a nearer to perfect execution of a performance. You can then go and physically attempt to express your thought form. Bearing in mind that studies have shown that vivid mental practice is as powerful as physical practice the mental preparation should provide you with a significant option to move forward.

● Thinking through a forthcoming competition can give you a sense of having been there before. This should take away some of the fears of the unknown. Something which realistically increases your feelings of security and self-confidence is going to help your stability and quality of performance. The stronger your self-confidence the more capable you will be of performing consistently. If your self-confidence outweighs your anxiety then your performance will not deteriorate in competition.

The Soviet Olympic sprint champion Valeri Borzov said that he used calming images before his heat and semi-final, but prior to his Olympic final he would relive highly successful experiences and he rehearsed winning. If you are in with a chance then this is a useful rehearsal. The images must be attainable for you, neither impossible nor too easy.

MENTAL REHEARSAL WITHIN A TEAM

There is a significant difference between individual and team sports. If you are a team member you can obviously use mental rehearsal to develop your individual skills, but your problem becomes considerably more complex when you add variables such as other team members and opponents.

British national hockey coach, David Whitaker, posed many 'What if..?' questions in his preparation of the men's team en route to their gold medal in Seoul. They gradually became more aware of the needs of their team-mates and what they were doing with their opponents. He asked them to become aware of patterns. It would be possible mentally to rehearse what you would do when certain player position patterns evolved. A great deal of discussion and discovery needs to take place to develop this level of awareness, but as this was Britain's first teamgame gold since 1936, the questioning process seems worth investigating!

It is quite common in team sports for a player to have his focus interrupted by a confrontation with an opponent. If this happens to you it is worth recalling that your actions follow your thoughts. If your mind is entirely occupied with seeking an opportunity to get an opponent back, then your focus of attention cannot be fully on performing at your best.

LEFT AND RIGHT
BRAIN BALANCE

In order to understand how better to achieve your potential, it should be useful to understand more of the predominantly different functions going on in the two halves of your brain. Although there is known to be an interchange between both sides of your brain, the understanding to date is that your left side is predominantly used for technical analysis. Information is processed sequentially in the left side of your brain. The logic of mathematics and language is processed with your left brain and you will tend to give yourself instruction and criticism based on the analytical information you have gathered.

Your right brain takes the sequential steps from the left brain and integrates them into a whole image. The end result is best described as a hologram. Intuition, creativity, spatial awareness and discovery are predominantly right brain functions. Action evolves from this right side.

When you were young your right brain will have been used to discover how you could walk and talk. Once you moved into secondary school, you and almost every other child in western society had to shift into predominantly left-brain thinking and work with the current bias of scientific, technical analysis of all things. So programmed are we all to this bias that after we have analysed and worked out the best goals for ourselves we often inhibit or sabotage our own actions by continually giving technical self-instruction and criticism, instead of simply executing the action. Our brain's left and right sides are sometimes actually competing for control. The key to appropriate focus is to use your left brain to gather information and work out what goal you want to achieve, then hand over control to the right brain to execute your actions. You can keep the left brain from interfering with its sequential instructions by focusing on the most noticeable sensation you experience in your action. If you can stay focused on your executing process as it happens, your action should maintain a flowing holistic form.

The bias of these mental chapters has been on your achieving more through thought. Let it be clearly understood that physical training will be no less required. Clarity of thought should encourage you to spend your time more productively. Your physical endeavour and joy of achievement is experienced through the process of reaching towards your potential, balancing and integrating your mind, body and spirit.

—————— *SUMMARY* ——————
Visualization and mental training

- **Visualization can decrease the tension associated with competition.**

- **Use your imagination to simulate competition conditions in training.**

- **Ensure that the focus of your awareness is appropriate.**

- **Allow the two sides of your brain to function in the areas to which they are best suited.**

4

HOW TO GET THE BEST FROM ADRENALIN

Guy Ogden

Top performers in any sport will say that they need the 'hype' of adrenalin to pull out a really good performance. Adrenalin is a hormone secreted from the adrenal glands just above each kidney. It has profound effects on the body's physiological processes. You will recognize many of these from experience. The changes which occur when adrenalin is secreted are a normal response to stress and prepare the body for fight or flight situations. Because it heightens physical performance to such a degree, the adrenal response explains why it is so difficult to achieve in training what is easily possible in competition. It may also explain the feeling of depression and lethargy which so often follows a major sporting achievement; when it goes, there is a sense of let-down. This sensation is not limited to athletes but seems to affect most 'performers'.

Adrenalin makes such a vital contribution that, without it, the performer is unable to produce more than a mediocre effort. You can prompt, control and heighten the adrenal response if you practise certain techniques in your preparation and training which include the mental rehearsal and visualization described in chapters 1-3. The aim of this chapter is to show you how to do this. However, you need to be aware that continued over-stimulation of the adrenal system can lead to exhaustion and loss of resistance to infection. Most top performers tread a very fine line between high achievement and breakdown of one kind or another. This chapter is also about the economy of the adrenal system; that is, how to get more out of it by preparation and training, while avoiding the excess demands which lead to breakdown.

To achieve this you need to learn how to limit the demands made on the system, while at the same time heightening the response.

HOW ADRENALIN WORKS

Adrenalin, when secreted into the blood-stream, has the following effects:

- It increases heart rate and blood pressure.
- It dilates blood vessels which supply major muscles.
- It raises levels of sugar and free fatty acids in the blood.
- It increases the rate and depth of breathing.
- It masks pain.
- It dilates the pupils of the eye.
- It facilitates sweating.
- It produces feelings of anxiety or apprehension (butterflies in the stomach, feeling 'keyed-up').

You can see that these responses are beneficial for the sports performer in that they mobilize and potentiate the systems of the body which will be called upon in a sports activity. The increase in blood supply to the major muscles will enhance co-ordination and the power of muscular contraction. On the mental level, adrenalin appears to increase powers of focus and concentration, and facilitates the kind of mental 'tunnel vision' required for a special performance. This may also result in an enhanced awareness and broad focus for team players.

The secretion of adrenalin can be provoked by physical and

mental stimuli. Traffic jams, coffee-drinking, music, troubled personal relationships, the sight of your rival competitor will all produce an adrenal response. Changing into sports gear and setting off to train will produce a significant rise in adrenalin. There is clearly a large number of circumstances and occasions in everyday life in which demands may be made on your adrenal system over and above the stress of competitive sport. It follows that you have to consider the overall stress levels in your life in planning the economy of the adrenal system.

Too much stress of different kinds for too long may impair your immune system and render you liable to minor ailments. The very high demands of peak performance in sport may be the 'last straw' that collapses an already overloaded system. Top performers are, by definition, high achievers, and this personality trait often entails high levels of adrenal demand. In planning a programme of preparation for peak performance, it pays to review your life outside the sport itself to assess the areas of stress to see if these can be reduced.

PRE-COMPETITION
MENTAL REHEARSAL AND RITUAL

You can heighten the adrenal response prior to competition by doing a kind of mental 'war dance'. Ideally, a ritual of preparation should be well established and practised in minor competition so that each item of the count-down is recognized and triggers a further boost to confirm the approaching demand.

For many performers this kind of ritual is included in the warm-up period before the event. It is not economic to try to sustain this heightened state of readiness for too long, although prior to the most important events the sensation of growing readiness may accumulate over a much longer period than normal. Distractions during the immediate pre-event period can be detrimental, not just to your physical, but also to your mental, preparation. A further important piece of advice: don't take input from anyone, not even your coach, at least ten minutes before your event. Immediately prior to the race or match is your time to get yourself in order and mentally to tune to the forthcoming focus.

In the 1986 Boston Marathon the invited overseas athletes were transported to the warm-up area at least two hours before the race was due to start. To avoid the kind of nervous pre-race encounters and milling around that usually occurs before these events I went off to a quiet place in a nearby forest and read a novel for an hour or so before starting my warm-up. I need about forty-five minutes to facilitate a fully heightened adrenal response and separating myself physically and mentally from the other athletes prevented unwanted distractions and protracted dissipation of energy in this vital pre-race count-down.

Competing in unfamiliar surroundings, perhaps in an alien culture and climate, has been known to disrupt even quite experienced performers. In these conditions, which are frequent for top performers, it is all the more important that you invoke the mental focus and tunnel vision of preparedness to protect against distraction. In team sports there may be value in organizing a collective ritual that provides for each player to 'go inside' and key in mentally to the task ahead. The point is that this is an intensely personal moment and the circumstances of team sports may not always provide that space.

The key factors are:

● You physically organize at the practical level all the equipment you require to avoid the disruption and distraction of the unfamiliar. This may involve carrying supplies of your favourite pre-competition food, drinks, music etc.

● You research and inform yourself as well as possible regarding the organization and timing of check-ins, reporting, warm-up facilities etc., so that you have a time-frame within which to carry out your final physical and mental preparation.
● You start a mental count-down aimed to climax at the start of competition. Each marker in the ritual of preparation can represent an increase in your confidence and invoke a feeling of control over your body, your mind, and the event itself.
● You mentally run through the whole performance.
● Use music. An inspiring piece of classical or popular music on a personal stereo can be used to aid concentration and increase the hype or provide the calm.
● You avoid or restrict interaction with fellow performers; it takes energy and focus away from your preparation.

TRAINING
AND COMPETITION PHASING

Training programmes and competition performances make mental demands on sports people. Many performers' programmes are designed with purely physical objectives in mind. I believe that top performers can improve their performances if a conscious planning effort is made to incorporate the mental conditioning aspect of preparation when designing both the training and competition programmes.

As with physical conditioning the mental demands need to be progressively increased with periods of recovery built into the programme. A mistake that many performers make is to treat each training session with the same degree of mental competitiveness that should belong to performance situations. Top performers vary greatly in how often they push themselves in training. Some, like Steve Ovett, never go to the limit, following the motto: 'train, don't strain'. Others, like

Herb Elliot, push themselves really hard for a part of every session. You must find out what works for you.

Do remember, the harder and more frequently you push, the shorter your career. Equally valid may be the idea that as you train you compete. If you never push yourself in training, how easy will it be for you to call for all-out effort in the competition?

Your training programme should distinguish stress sessions from recovery sessions in a mental as well as a physical sense. The mental concentration, self-awareness and commitment required of an intensively stressful work-out is demanding on the adrenal system, and requires a recovery period to follow it so that greater demands can be made on the next occasion.

By making moderately high demands at every training session the system is not sufficiently stressed to make the adaptive response required for top performance, and yet it is being steadily worn down over a period of time. The chronic fatigue which some performers complain of is both mental and physical, and is not productive.

The adrenal system can be primed in such a way that the training programme results in a performer who is mentally 'hungry' for the event at the start of the performance.

Enthusiasm is vital to good performance. Use this as your guide. If the intensity of your training is killing your enthusiasm then you need to reduce either the quantity or quality, or both.

It is suggested that this aspect of conditioning and preparation should be organized as follows:

TRAINING

Training programmes must distinguish between stress and recovery sessions. In stress sessions you approach the work

with a high degree of concentration, you 'associate' throughout the session with what is going on, you 'read' the body,
mentally conscious of body positioning, tension, fatigue, etc.
As far as possible you simulate the focus required of a performance situation. This is a high cost session in terms of
mental energy, and should leave you feeling as tired as if you
had worked intensely.

In the recovery sessions which follow a stress session you
try to 'dissociate' from the activity, focus on letting go or focus
on recovery in the muscles. This is a light workout involving
no sensation of mental effort. The body goes through the
motions, and you relax and enjoy the feeling of working out in
a playful and recreational way. During this period of recovery
the neuromuscular co-ordination and circulation are kept
primed, but the body and mind are building up resources for
the next stress session which will make further demands on a
strengthened system. The chart below shows the recommended pattern.

PATTERN OF STRESS-RECOVERY
IN TRAINING PROGRAMMES

STRESS	RECOVERY	STRESS	RECOVERY	STRESS	RECOVERY
High intensity or volume work-out		Competition		High intensity or volume work-out	

NB. The recovery sessions should represent at least twice the number of stress sessions, particularly following competitive performance, or very high intensive or high
volume workouts. This will minimize injury or sickness while still improving performance.

COMPETITION

The demands of maximal effort in competitive performance are both physical and mental. In planning a season it is realistic to set primary and secondary goals, so that a series of major performances leads towards the major performance of the season. Between these efforts, periods of recovery training will allow the body and mind to restore the energy and enthusiasm required for subsequent demands. After the major performance effort you should ideally have an extended period of recovery.

It is difficult to arrive at the kind of condition that top performers achieve when at the peak of fitness. It is even more difficult to sustain this condition for long. The 'rules of recovery' should enable performers to maintain condition longer, if the emphasis in planning switches from concern about the intensity of training efforts to concern about recovery rates and the extent to which the performer is ready for further stress sessions, and what kind of stress sessions these should be.

Most performers do not have available to them the sophisticated and highly specialized medical laboratory facilities which, through analysis of blood samples and muscle biopsy, would give them more precise indications of fatigue and recovery. It is necessary, therefore, to work from a kind of 'ready reckoner' system which will ensure sufficient margins of safety to maximize potential and minimize the likelihood of breakdown. The ready reckoner will be personal to the athlete but based upon the signs of overuse that are listed in chapter 10. In addition, the system of training programmes based on recovery periods is also a ready-reckoner in that you apply it routinely without recourse to physiological tests. A substantial part of such a system must be the performer's own subjective feelings and awareness of the physiological processes involved in attaining peak condition.

Whilst emphasizing the importance of recovery in this system, the top performer's need to push beyond previous limits in both training and competition cannot be neglected. This system and the training programmes outlined in chapter 12 provide for this need and ensure that the performer can explore the unknown territory of new personal records in training sessions and competition.

With this kind of combined mental and physical phasing of effort the expectation is that the performers will be able to sustain sessions of higher intensity and volume than with systems that incorporate inadequate periods of recovery. The limitations on making maximal demands on the body are, in our opinion, generally more mental than physical. Training the adrenal system therefore becomes a key part of the overall preparation for maximal demands.

DE-STRESSING:
HOW TO REDUCE ADRENAL OVERUSE

Everyday life in the modern world provides numerous occasions for the alarm response of the adrenal system to be activated. Limiting those occasions to produce your top performance is very important as the system needs to be primed and responsive to the very high demands that will be made upon it in competition.

We have encountered performers in several fields of sport who have experienced a type of 'burn-out' syndrome following a combination of major physical and mental demands. Frequently the syndrome defies orthodox medical diagnosis, but it is characterized by an all-pervading fatigue and low resistance to infection. The performer suffering in this way may embark on a training programme only to encounter some kind of breakdown in health at a very early stage in the build-up period. The fatigue and depression can be extremely debilitating.

Although there is as yet no direct medical evidence to connect this kind of event to the adrenal system, those who succumb to the condition are high achievers who make constant high demands on their systems. As with other physiological factors that may affect methods of training, preparation and performance, it is not possible to wait for final medical proof before making planning decisions in respect of training programmes. There is sufficient clinical and common experience to suggest the wisdom of building prevention and avoidance of physical overuse and mental fatigue into the programme from the beginning.

In addition to the advice on the phasing of training and competition in the previous section, three other areas of de-stressing action might be suggested:

1   Review of key areas in the performer's life outside sport

2   The use of relaxation techniques

3   Avoidance of known dietary stressors

——— 1 ———

REVIEW OF KEY AREAS
IN THE PERFORMER'S LIFE OUTSIDE SPORT

Although there are numerous examples of top performers achieving goals against the odds of all kinds of personal difficulty, this approach is concerned with the maximization of adrenal response in a specifically sporting context. It follows that, in advocating an economy of the adrenal system, it is advisable to look for ways to decrease the demand on the system in other parts of a performer's life. This by no means precludes simultaneous high levels of demand and achievement in, for example, career or study, as many top performers have demonstrated. We can distinguish between stress that is chosen, contained within the framework of overall aims and priorities in a person's life, and stress that is experienced as imposed from outside, and is not perceived as part of the overall plan. The second type of 'out-of-control' stress is a subtraction from the available energy pool and leads to a diminished adrenal capability in the long-term.

You might, for example, alter your feeling of irritation at limited time or facilities for training. Look at your attitude, recognize that you have choices, evaluate your options and make your commitment. You might, for example, see the possibilities for other kinds of preparation, or the positive advantage of avoiding over-training. It pays to adopt a recreational activity which makes the minimum of physical and mental demands, which takes the performer away from the sport, and which can be carried out on recovery days or employed consciously in preventing too much stressful mental preoccupation with the sport. In other words, provided that the performer's total stress levels are acceptable, it may be a positive advantage not to be a 'full-time' sportsperson.

—— 2 ——
THE USE OF RELAXATION TECHNIQUES

Many top performers have discovered the value of using one or other of the better known forms of relaxation technique in their preparation. The point of using such methods is to reduce the generally aggravated state of alarm response which many people come to regard as a normal state of being. Reducing stress levels in this way not only 'rests' the adrenal system but also clears the mind for a more efficiently focused concentration when required. It enables the performer to clear the distraction of background 'noise' in the head when preparing for performance. There are techniques similar to transcendental meditation or the meditation used in yoga that can be acquired in a short time to a level that can be effective when applied to sports performance situations. It is recommended that performers spend a short time each day using some form of relaxation technique as part of their training and preparation programme. This period can also be used to carry out some of the positive visualization techniques described in chapters 1 and 3.

—— 3 ——
AVOIDANCE OF KNOWN DIETARY STRESSORS

Sensitivity to foods is becoming more common. Many people are mildly allergic to foods without realizing it. Paradoxically it is often the foods to which you are most addicted that you are allergic to. The reason for this is that the allergic response triggers the adrenal system which gives you a sensation of 'lift' or well-being. The classic craving for a cup of tea or coffee is an example of this.

Wheat products, dairy foods, chocolate and caffeine (tea, coffee) are the worst offenders in the list of potentially allergic foodstuffs. Sometimes the symptoms of sensitivity are apparent, as in a stuffy nose, skin reactions, headaches, etc. But more important from the point of view of top performance are sub-clinical sensitivities where the allergy subtracts from the performer's general level of energy and well-being. In these cases the performer may be unaware of the extent to which the adrenal system is under constant dietary siege. The symptoms of chronic fatigue may have as much to do with an eating pattern as with a training programme. As with fatigue and recovery, athletes and coaches have no easy access to precise means of measuring allergic response to foods, although some standard skin reaction tests are available in allergy-testing clinics.

With food sensitivity in the sports performance context we need to ensure that the performer minimizes the possible deleterious effects of potential allergens in food. The best way to do this is to organize the diet along some safety guidelines. More information about diet for performance is to be found in chapter 5.

Here are the guidelines for avoiding long-term dietary stress:

● Avoid caffeine-containing products like tea, coffee and chocolate, or at least limit their use to the earlier part of the day (they interfere with sleep patterns).
● Take wheat-containing foods only at one meal in the same day. For example, if you have a wheat-based cereal and toast for breakfast, do not follow this with sandwiches for lunch and pasta in the evening.
● Limit your intake of dairy-products of all kinds (including beef). Eliminating them entirely from the diet is not difficult as vegetable-based substitutes can be easily obtained.
● Wherever possible, avoid the use of foods containing additives, high concentrations of refined sugar, colouring agents and preservatives.

These general rules will minimize the stress that foods can cause to the performer who is trying to maximize performance.

────── *SUMMARY* ──────

How to use
the adrenal system effectively

To heighten the response:

● **Mentally label each training session as 'stress' or 'recovery'.**

- Mentally rehearse the activity to key-in the appropriate response to effort.

- Use focused, associative concentration in the stress sessions.

- Use pre-competition rituals in the final hours before performance to build up the adrenal response in a controlled way.

- Phase and limit the competitive demands of your total programme with seasonal targets sufficiently spaced out to give the adrenal system a chance to recover.

To limit the demands:

- Dissociate mentally from the activity during recovery sessions and simply go through the motions without any sensation of mental effort.

- Use periods of relaxation to focus on letting go of effort and strain. Use any method of inducing a state of relaxation in the muscles. A flotation chamber, if you have access to one, can be very useful for this.

- Programme rest days with activities that take your mind completely off your sport.

- Minimize as far as possible the other stresses in your life style or take measures to counteract them, e.g. by using meditation, yoga or relaxation techniques, for a period each day.

- Reduce the use of stimulants in your diet, particularly caffeine; avoid food additives and high concentrations of refined sugar.

- Plan the training and performance schedule so that recovery is adequate between maximal demands.

5

EATING
FOR
PERFORMANCE

Guy Ogden

There is no magic food that will enhance performance. The differences in dietary habits between performers are very wide indeed. If you were to check on what the finalists in a single Olympic event were in the habit of eating the variation would be staggering. Top performers are good at their sport primarily because of their mental approach, their training and their mental application, not because of what they eat. They may believe that certain foods enhance performance but the effect of this is more on their confidence than on the chemistry of energy.

This is not to say that diet is unimportant. In recent years a vast amount of literature has appeared on diet and nutritional requirements so that the ordinary citizen is bombarded almost daily with some new finding of importance. Sportspeople have not escaped the attentions of the manufacturers of dietary supplements. The difficulty is to find a balanced position between grasping at everything new and closing the mind to possibly useful information.

Inadequate diets or excesses of any kind can certainly limit and diminish performance or may lead to a nutritional status where the performer is infection- or injury-prone. So in this chapter we will be looking at ways to minimize the risks of limiting performance by poor eating habits. We will look at the dietary needs created by high levels of physical exercise and the conditions that surround top performers. This is another area where the individual performer has to take a high degree of personal responsibility based upon reliable information.

The general recommendations for diet are not substantially different for sportspeople than for anyone else but there are special considerations to bear in mind, apart from the obviously greater amount of energy expended in programmes of training. High levels of physical effort are accompanied by high fluid losses. Water-soluble vitamins may be used and lost in greater quantities. Both men and women performers should be aware of the possibility of iron deficiency anaemia when undergoing periods of heavy training. Top performers who have to travel long distances to competition venues may have to contend not only with unfamiliar food but also the effects of jet lag. All these factors mean that, as a top performer, serious thought has to be given to nutrition as a part of thorough preparation.

It is also important to avoid becoming obsessed with food or over-dependent on special diets that may be difficult to arrange when travelling. The anxiety caused by not having the 'right' foods is bad for confidence. Most top performers will have a routine pre-competition meal which they know suits them and will often ensure that the right foods are available by taking supplies with them. . . . but, apart from stomach upsets that may be caused by food or water, the limitations on your performance which can be related to food are to do with your overall nutritional status, not with what you ate just before you competed.

Particular sports will often have associated attitudes to food based upon the performers' perceptions of the required physical and energy profile of the sport. The weight-lifter favours a relatively high-protein intake and the marathon runner craves carbohydrates. These perceptions can lead to food habits that are not necessarily beneficial. In this chapter we will look critically at some of the practices that have become established patterns among performers.

PLANNING A BALANCED DIET

There is a short-term and a long-term issue concerning sports nutrition. The short-term issue is ensuring sufficient energy for the training or competitive performance. The long-term issue has to do with protection from infection and injury, recovery from maximum effort and the responsiveness of the body to training stresses. If your body is not receiving sufficient food as fuel you will not be able to perform effectively. So there is a simple input-output equation which must be balanced. Not all foods are equally useful as primary fuel and so some foods are to be recommended more than others.

The long-term health and efficiency of the sporting body will depend on adequate absorption of micronutrients like vitamins and minerals. Unfortunately, we still know too little about how individuals' requirements of these micronutrients vary and what extra needs may be occasioned by sustained heavy training. Recommended Daily Allowances (RDAs) are a guide that many nutritionists regard as minimal. Experience suggests that individuals may be subclinically deficient in specific micronutrients. This means that, whilst they show no overt signs or symptoms of deficiency, they may be disadvantaged in their response to training efforts or in healing time when injured. As with other aspects of sports physiology we cannot wait for research to provide us with all the evidence before taking planning decisions with today's performers.

Planning a diet that will lead to the best health and sports performance is not like planning other aspects of a training programme because eating habits and food preferences are highly individual and often have emotional or symbolic significance. Changing eating patterns is not just a matter of providing factual information about food. Sportspeople are no different from others in their liking for certain foods and feeling better on some diets rather than others. It is advisable to review your diet by keeping a record of everything you eat and drink over a typical week and comparing it with the recommendations set out in this chapter. Try to bring your eating habits closer into line with these recommendations by degrees rather than attempting to make sudden drastic changes. The basic pattern of eating over a substantial period of time is what influences your health and potential performance, not a fad diet carried out for a few weeks.

The ideal diet would consist of fresh foods, picked or harvested ripe and consumed close to the source of production. This, however, is not realistic for the urban dweller. The best we can do, given the way food is produced and marketed, is to eat foods that have been processed or altered as little as possible. This means a heavy emphasis in the basic diet on fresh fruits, salads, wholegrain cereals, fish, uncooked and lightly-cooked vegetables.

The highly processed foods have the disadvantage of containing, among other additives, high levels of sodium (salt) and sugar. These can interfere with blood sugar levels and fluid balance in the body. Animal products nowadays undergo considerable additions in the form of artificial feeds, hormones for growth and antibiotics for combating disease. Some of these will be present in the final product and it may be wise to limit your intake of meat and poultry and to substitute fish whenever possible.

WHAT TO EAT FOR FUEL

The best way to provide muscles with the energy they need is to eat carbohydrate-rich foods. This source of energy is readily absorbed by the body with waste products of carbon-dioxide and water which are easily eliminated. Most performers need no persuasion to eat carbohydrates as they crave them. The problem is that often they favour them in the form of refined and concentrated sugary snacks. This plays havoc with the regulation of blood sugar in the body. You can create a sensitivity to these foods so that the pattern of your blood sugar during the day is a series of peaks and troughs. If a trough occurs during a training session it will severely limit your ability to exercise.

The latest research suggests that you should take in about 500 grams of carbohydrate a day. The form this takes may vary but should consist mainly of fresh or dried fruit, rice, potatoes, fresh vegetables and wholegrain cereals. These natural sources of carbohydrate are also associated with minerals, vitamins and trace elements which are a useful contribution to your diet. Five hundred grams of carbohydrate would have to be achieved over the whole day's food intake from a variety of sources. A sample day might include breakfast: wholegrain cereal 70 gms, wholegrain bread or toast and honey 100 gms, fresh fruit (banana) 30 gms; lunch: baked potato 50 gms, salad (including beetroot and carrot) 20 gms, dried fruit 60 gms; evening meal: rice and vegetables 100 gms, dessert 70 gms. If you do not take in sufficient carbohydrate you risk poor recovery from your stress sessions of training as your muscles will not restore essential reserves of glycogen (the fuel for muscle contraction).

The problem with the appetite for carbohydrate is the tendency to satisfy it with sugary snacks and refined flour products. This habit can lead to a system that is reactive to sugar so that blood glucose levels follow an erratic pattern of highs and lows throughout the day as you try to lift your energy level with a cup of tea or coffee and a snack every so often. This state is bad for anyone, but particularly for sportspeople who need to make major physical demands on their bodies. To avoid it you should try to start the day with a reasonable protein component to your breakfast. Skimmed milk, soya protein supplement as a drink, or the occasional boiled egg will help to sustain a more even level of blood sugar through the day.

In the past, before the science of nutrition was based upon research evidence, it was thought that athletes and sportspeople needed extra quantities of protein to sustain their activities. We now know that this is not true and that the primary need is for extra carbohydrate to fuel our physical output. But in advocating this pattern of eating there is a danger that performers may acquire a form of hypoglycaemia (low blood sugar). Those endurance athletes who have experienced 'hitting the wall' show symptoms of low blood sugar, not of glycogen depletion in the muscles. I recall that on several occasions I suffered from hypoglycaemia in the course of a distance event after a high carbohydrate pre-race meal – which is precisely what most of the authorities advocate. In the 1986 Boston Marathon I ate a fairly high-protein pre-race meal and had the most comfortable marathon of my career.

The problem with research findings is that when they are popularized they encourage people to make extreme changes. This is particularly true where food facts are concerned. We do not advocate a return to huge T-bone steaks nor do we recommend taking the high-protein supplements that are among the latest sports food fads. But some cautionary points about the balance of carbohydrate and protein within a generally high-carbohydrate diet are worth making. In spite of the now general assumption that the body does not react to complex (unrefined) carbohydrates, some research suggests that the picture is not so simple. One study showed that blood sugar changes depended upon the type of carbohydrate – bread as opposed to rice or potatoes – and not just upon whether it is complex or refined. The only sure way to limit hypoglycaemic reactions is to balance protein intake, particularly at the start of the day. Include some protein in your breakfast (e.g. a boiled egg or soya supplement) as this helps to keep the blood sugar up through the morning.

FOODS TO AVOID

Food intolerance is becoming more commonly recognized and many people are aware of being sensitive to certain classes of foods. The symptoms of food sensitivity range from skin conditions, catarrhal conditions, headaches, hyperactivity, respiratory problems and so on. Allergies are commonly associated with dairy foods, wheat (or gluten-containing) products, eggs, chocolate, wine, coffee and food additives and preservatives. This is far from a complete list. Symptoms of intolerance can likewise be mild and take the form of lethargy and fatigue.

To restate an observation made in chapter 4, a seeming paradox is that you may be addicted to the foods that you have an allergy to. This is because your body responds with alarm to the intake of the offending food and secretes adrenalin which you experience as a lift, a temporary sense of well-being. In between intakes you feel tired and lacking in energy. Low blood sugar (hypoglycaemia) is often a result of addiction to caffeine-containing drinks (coffee, cola, tea) and addiction to concentrated refined carbohydrates such as chocolate bars, biscuits and buns.

Sportspeople are generally advised to consume more complex, unrefined carbohydrates to provide the fuel for high-output programmes of training. While we would agree in principle with this advice we would caution against eating large quantities of wheat-based foods at more than one meal a day. This is because you can create a food sensitivity by consuming too much of it over a period of time. Wholegrain bread is a good source of energy but should be used at only one meal per day. Therefore, if you have wheat-based muesli or wholemeal toast at breakfast, do not have sandwiches at lunch and pasta in the evening.

The pre-marathon pasta party has become a feature of many of the top international marathons. People are encouraged to consume large quantities of, often wholemeal, pasta. This supplies a quantity of roughage that often has to be eliminated at various pit-stops along the marathon route the next day. It would be preferable to go for foods that leave relatively little residue prior to competition, particularly as pre-race nerves more or less guarantee bowel movements. Ideal foods might be white rice, lean meat, fish, omelette, potato (any kind) and ice cream. This all means a reduction in heavy fibre intake.

FLUID BALANCE

In normal training and competition, thirst is a very poor indicator of fluid requirements and it is a good idea to develop the habit of taking fluid supplies along to training sessions and competitions. Take frequent small quantities, regardless of thirst. In dry, windy conditions you can dehydrate without realizing it, as your sweat evaporates quickly leaving the skin dry. A useful indicator of the state of fluid balance is the colour of your urine. A darker colour indicates a more concentrated urine and the need to take in more fluid. Endurance sportspeople particularly should ensure that their urine is as clear as water before the start of the event.

Replacement fluids that contain various concentrations of glucose, and minerals such as potassium, sodium and magnesium, are commercially available and are often supplied by the organisers of major events. The important fact to understand is that the more concentrated the solution, the more slowly will the fluid be absorbed from the stomach. So a very sweet drink could actually promote dehydration. Very small quantities of minerals (electrolytes) appear to speed up the absorption of fluid from the stomach. You need to find a balanced formula that suits you and ensure that you start to replace lost fluid long before you feel thirsty.

Jet lag is a factor that many top performers must contend with these days. Dehydration is one of the outcomes of air travel. Try to avoid any alcohol or coffee during the flight and take extra fluid in the form of fruit juices or water. Another tip to reduce the effects of jet lag is to ensure a good supply of potassium to the body; this can be found in bananas, dried fruit and potato skins.

SUPPLEMENTS
OF VITAMINS AND MINERALS

The body requires amounts of vitamins and minerals which are determined by the individual functioning of the system. This means that different individuals may need different amounts of the same vitamin. We have as yet no way of determining exactly how much of each kind any individual may need. Nutritionists work with Recommended Daily Allowances (RDAs) and some naturopaths use megadoses of vitamins which greatly exceed RDAs.

There is no doubt that a vitamin or mineral deficiency will

impair performance and can result in susceptibility to injury and slow healing. If your diet is poor in B and C vitamins or if you are iron-deficient your performance may suffer. Some performers may be subclinically deficient, in the sense not of actually having clinical symptoms, but of lacking sufficient resources to undergo intensive training programmes. If your diet is heavily biased towards processed and refined foods and you are under constant stress you may be heading for such a deficiency. The first step should be to get your basic diet along the right lines, as no amount of supplementation is a substitute for a bad diet.

If you do decide to supplement your diet with vitamins or minerals be careful to take balanced formulas. If you take an excess of one vitamin or mineral you can inhibit the absorption of another one. A balanced B vitamin formula will ensure that you get all the B group in the correct proportions so that this unintended effect does not happen.

Iron deficiency anaemia is not uncommon among both male and female athletes. Unexplained loss of form, fatigue and poor sleeping patterns could indicate this condition. It is better to get a blood test to determine exactly the nature of the problem and then decide what supplementation or dietary changes are needed. Sometimes, intakes are adequate in RDA terms but losses are excessive as, for example, with abnormally high menstrual bleeding. Iron is notoriously poorly absorbed from dietary sources and often supplementation is essential.

Some recent research suggests that dedicated female performers may suffer bone density losses as a result of the hormonal changes associated with weight loss and stopping ovulation and menstruation (amenorrhoea). There are risks of stress fractures occurring more regularly in female performers who undergo these changes.

If you deliberately restrict food intake in order to keep your weight down your diet may be low in calcium and contribute to this problem. Contrary to popular opinion, the calcium in dairy foods may not always be well absorbed, especially in cases of dairy food intolerance. You do not have to eat a lot of cheese and milk products. Leafy green vegetables, raw green salads (not just lettuce, but dandelion, collards, kale etc.) with a lemon or vinegar dressing, sprouted beans and seeds, almonds, brazil and hazel nuts all provide a rich source of available calcium without the risks associated with increasing animal fat intake. Chocolate and coffee inhibit calcium absorption, so avoid the high-energy snack habit.

Exercise-associated amenorrhoea that lasts for more than six months should be medically investigated to ensure that there is not a more serious underlying disorder.

WEIGHT AND PERFORMANCE

Gross weight is the sum of all the tissues of the body – bone, muscle, fat and fluids – and therefore does not tell you anything about the ratio of, say, fat to lean muscle. You can gain gross weight on an exercise programme as you reduce fat and increase muscle mass. You would look thinner, feel fitter but could weigh more. For most events there is probably something to be gained by reducing weight to the minimum consistent with the strength and power requirements of the sport. In endurance events extra weight is a positive disadvantage. But optimum weight is an individual matter and some people find that reducing beyond a certain level has negative results and leads to fatigue and loss of strength. We do not recommend dieting alone as a way of losing weight but following the dietary guidelines in this chapter and a training programme of progressive intensity should ensure that body weight approaches the optimum. Cutting out the sugary snacks and drinks and taking smaller meals in conjunction with a prog-ramme of training should be effective. Vegetarians often over-consume dairy foods so if weight is a problem cut back (but not cut out) these foods.

Some performers find that their weight will rise in fallow, off-season periods and then gradually approach optimum 'rac-ing weight' as the training intensifies and the competitive sea-son approaches. This kind of rhythm may be beneficial as it means that the performer is not trying to sustain that peak of condition for too great a part of the year and is allowing time for recovery and repair.

Some performers report increased flexibility as a conse-quence of weight loss. This may, in part, be due to reduction in the fat packing around the major joints and is an added bonus but, unless you are clearly overweight, do not try to improve your flexibility in this way as you will probably be disap-pointed.

—————— *SUMMARY* ——————
How to eat for
performance

- **Eat a diet that emphasizes fresh, natural foods.**

- **Reduce the chances of food intolerance by not eating one class of food excessively.**

- **Cut out the non-foods such as coffee, tea and alcohol and also refined and processed foods.**

- **Ensure adequate protein intake to counteract hypo-glycaemic tendencies.**

- Keep weight to the minimum consistent with the strength and power requirements of your sport.

- Use vitamin and mineral supplements only in balanced formulas and not in megadoses, unless prescribed.

- Female performers in particular should be aware of the symptoms of iron deficiency anaemia.

- Calcium should be ingested to combat bone problems associated with amenorrhoea.

- Take particular care with diet at times of injury, major training or competitive stress.

- Take care with fluid replacement before, during and after training or competition.

6

HOW TO ENHANCE EFFICIENCY AND ENERGY FLOW THROUGH THE BODY

Guy Ogden

There is an elegance about the movement of a top performer in action. It has much to do with economy of movement. The accomplished performer appears to move effortlessly; maximum power is produced with the minimum of resistance. There are no wasted movements; the body appears to move around a central axis located somewhere between the navel and the solar plexus. You can see this most clearly in gymnasts and dancers but it is there to a greater or lesser extent in the top performers in any sport. This chapter is about ways of working towards this kind of perfection of movement.

The energy that is generated in a body used in this way appears to flow through the movements unblocked by distortions of posture or tension. You can see this in photographs of finishing line movements where the winner is caught breasting the tape with perfect form while the rest of the field displays varying degrees of effort, strain and distortion of style. To achieve this perfection of form you need to work on a mental and physical level. The visual image and physical awareness of your body in action is as important to this development as the routines of stretching and strengthening which you have to undergo to impove the use of your limbs.

The technique of improvement is based upon the methods described in the chapters on mental preparation. You begin by becoming aware of where things are. Much of the correction and adjustment will occur simply as a result of directing attention to key areas which have major control over the way you use your body.

Although we associate running and jumping with the legs, throwing with the arms and skiing with arms and legs, from an osteopathic point of view the key area in all types of body use is the spine. How efficiently you move is largely determined by what your spine will allow. In many of us there are areas of restricted movement which mean that we cannot sidebend or rotate the spine sufficiently. Another aspect of reduced efficiency is the outcome of postural or emotional factors which result in distortions of the normal curves of the spine. Tension and holding in the neck and head area displaces the centre of gravity and reduces the amount of overall rotation in the spine.

A certain amount of energy is used up simply in maintaining these patterns of holding. But, apart from economy, these distortions detract from the smooth flow of energy through the body in motion. Try running flat out while clenching your teeth as hard as possible to experience the effect of tension in distant areas of the body on performance. Our experience is that the key to relaxed and efficient energy flow is the position and state of tension of the head and neck and a major part of this chapter will be devoted to what you can do to improve your habits in this area.

The objective is to arrive at an effortless, balanced use of the body that allows maximum power with minimum resistance, as in martial arts or dance. Every sport has its unique requirements and you will need to apply the principles and the method to your particular event. As with the other aspects of conditioning described in this book, we are looking at ways in which you can remove internal obstacles to maximizing your natural potential.

How to Get
More Length in Your Spine

Thought affects body use. We describe someone as having a weight on their mind, carrying the world on their shoulders, looking hunted. These phrases convey an image of posture. The spine in these postures, from an osteopathic standpoint, has been compressed or shortened. This compression occurs in the course of dealing with emotions like fear or anger which are withheld. Muscles contract and stay shortened long after the original stress has been removed.

The body tends to become more contracted and compressed with increasing age. This process has an effect on energy flow through the body. Disciplines like tai-chi, yoga and the Alexander technique counteract this tendency to shorten and compress. Osteopathic treatment helps by lengthening and adjusting the balance of muscles responsible for this shortening process. It may be very useful at the start of the process in helping to remove restrictions and tightness in the spine which would prevent you from getting the most from your active programme of stretching.

To lengthen the spine, you will need to work on physical stretching of the muscles and soft tissues that have shortened and you will need to visualize the spine lengthening and freeing as you train in your particular sport. It is a good idea to use the recovery sessions in the programme to rehearse the progressive development of style that this involves. This point is slightly counter to the concept of disassociation, although the amount of practice this style change requires may only amount to one recovery session in three or so. Also, the mode of exploration is playful rather than focused in a stress session sense. The experience of this session would not be one of effort, but the results of it may be highly significant for long-term development. The help of a coach or training partner with or without a video can be especially useful in providing you with feedback on this development.

Start this development by committing a recovery training session to exploring where things are for you. Begin by reporting back to yourself any awareness of tension, heaviness or pain. Then go through the whole body from head to toe noting what you can about the state of each level. Remember that you are not trying to alter anything at this stage; you are simply increasing your awareness of where things are. You could use this kind of self questioning:

● How does my head feel? Is it heavy or light? Is it held forward or back? Does it move more to one side than the other? Is my jaw clenched or loose? How loose on a scale of 1–10 – if 10 is perfectly relaxed?
● How do my shoulders feel? Is one held tighter than the other? Can I move my shoulders freely or is there a feeling of restriction? How loose do they feel on a scale of 1–10 – if 10 is perfectly relaxed?

If you use this kind of schedule of self-questioning you will find that some beneficial adjustments will happen automatically. In distance running, for example, I have always used this kind of mental run-through the body from top to toe in the course of competitive performances. Bringing your attention to the various parts of the body as you are in action will help to relax them and you may not need to do any more than this. A coach can use this method with individuals or groups by asking them to focus on an aspect of body position during a part of the session and then to report back on it afterwards.

The progression from the awareness exercise is achieved by experimenting with different positions. Try exaggerating a tendency like holding the head too far back to experience what it does to your action. It can be entertaining and instructive to feel the effects of faulty style magnified in this way.

Most of the tension we hold in the spine starts in the neck and shoulders. The muscles at the back of the neck tend to draw the head back and down to the shoulders. To release this tension lie on your back, on a carpet, with your knees bent and a telephone book under the back of your head. Relax in that position and feel the muscles lengthen at the back of the neck. You may need to adjust the thickness of the telephone book to get the best results. You should try to let the knees fall inwards rather than outwards and may need to place the feet further apart to achieve this. It is a good idea to start your stretching routine with this relaxation technique as it tunes the body into a lengthening mode.

To get a little further with lengthening the spine you can use a yoga position called 'the plough'. You can make it easy to begin with by taking a chair to support your legs. You lie full length on your back on the floor with your head about a foot from a chair. Bring your legs up with bent knees and push your back off the floor with your hands. Straighten your legs and bring them to rest on the chair. Relax in this position and feel the stretch from between the shoulders up the back of your neck. Progression from this is achieved by stretching without the chair. Try gradually to straighten the legs and you should feel the stretch running from behind the neck all the way down to the achilles tendon. This position should be sustained for a few minutes each day to get the best results.

HEAD AND NECK POSITION:
RELAXATION IS THE KEY
TO EFFICIENCY

The head leads and controls movement. See what the effect of turning and looking over your shoulder is on your direction and speed in running. Try carrying out any normal movement in your sport with your head held in an unfamiliar position. The influence the head has over movement is even more profound than you will have experienced with these simple distortions. As the head is the heaviest part of the body it has to be delicately balanced on the spine. The muscles that support the position of the head also register mental tension or stress. Many performers carry postural distortions into their sporting activity. I have often observed top performers with considerable neck and shoulder tension and wondered how much better they might be if they were to work on freeing up that area of their spines.

Ideally, the intention or will to initiate an action or effort comes from the head but the *energy* for that action comes from the centre of the body. Watch a top performer respond to a tactical move in a game of tennis or a track race and compare the action, particularly in terms of what happens to the head, with that of a lesser performer. The response in a top performer does not lead to a contraction in the neck and shoulder region. Lesser performers appear to displace energy too high in the body so that it appears as if the intention and the energy to carry out the movement come from the same source. In running, I found that a horizon that was too high, involving looking too far ahead, was as bad as running with the eyes focusing too close to the feet. The ideal body position results from an almost straight line from the back of the head through the hips and down to the heel when the leg is fully extended. The access to this improvement is through changes in the way you hold your head, not in focusing on the trunk or lower limb. Slow-motion film of 100 metre finalists shows how the whole body at maximum effort moves powerfully under a head that appears to be almost perfectly still. Look at slow shots of a high jumper to see how the head is used to initiate movement and change of direction. You can learn a lot by looking at top performers in action to see how these aspects of body-use enhance or limit their movement.

If you have a neck and shoulder area that is very restricted you may benefit from some deep massage and osteopathic mobilization to get you started. Then a routine of regular stretching will give you the mobility to experiment with different head positions. The aim is for a lighter, more balanced position where the supporting muscles have only to make minor adjusting movements, rather than holding the whole weight of the head under constant strain. You should be able to rotate the head to each side with the shoulders still so that your chin is in line with the point of each shoulder. If you cannot do this without a sensation of pulling or strain you need to lengthen the muscles around the neck. You should also be able to bring your chin to your chest and to sidebend your head to bring the ears close to the shoulder. If you work on these neck mobility movements you will be surprised to see how much freer the body becomes as the centre of gravity is restored closer to the navel.

HOW TO RELEASE
TENSION IN THE JAW

When a physical effort starts to hurt we often speak of the need to 'grit the teeth' and carry on. This is poor advice. Clenching the jaw or gritting the teeth has a weakening effect on the power of contraction in the muscles of the body. The latest research on the temporo-mandibular joint, which is the joint between the lower jaw and the upper jaw, suggests that distortions of tension in this area have far-reaching effects on muscle function in the rest of the body. The balance of the jaw can be altered by habitual tension in the local muscles as well as by dental problems.

Some performers are noted for a tendency to grimace and contract the muscles of the neck at extremes of effort. This is usually accompanied by drawing the head back and down. To release more available energy you should consciously tilt the head slightly forward and relax the jaw and emphasize breathing out forcefully rather than breathing in.

In warm-up activities you should spend some time on letting go of any nervous tension accumulated around the face, jaw and neck. Head rotation, stretching the jaw wide and releasing, and sharp exhalation with loose lips, are all useful ways of getting this area of the body relaxed and ready for effort. In training sessions you should practise maximum and sub-maximum efforts with relaxed jaw muscles so that your body responds to stress with a reflex to relax rather than to tense up.

Breathing out to access a more powerful muscle contraction is well known in martial arts and weight-lifting sports but less commonly applied elsewhere. A sharp exhalation of breath can be used to initiate a change of pace and helps you to increase effort without increasing tension.

ROTATION IS THE KEY
TO FREER MOVEMENT

Although most top performers have by now accepted the need for stretching routines as part of complete preparation, this often does not go beyond simple remedial lengthening of the muscles most used in the particular sport. So cyclists will stretch front thigh and calf muscles and hurdlers will work on their hamstrings. The limitations on performances can be pushed back even further if the spine is able to rotate more freely, particularly for athletics and sports involving running movement of any kind.

The limitations on spinal rotation are mainly soft tissues that support the bony skeleton, that is, muscles, ligaments, and connective tissues called fascias which bind areas in sheet-like bands. Simple linear muscle stretches are important but not enough to reach the complex binding structures which are the real limitation on the body in motion.

You can improve your overall mobility by stretching the fascia and to do this you need to introduce some rotation elements into your stretching routine. As these fascial bands link the upper and lower body, some of the positions come to resemble yoga positions. Some performers have found yoga a very helpful addition to their preparation. You can find the main stretches recommended in the final chapter of this book but you can be creative in inventing your own stretches. Everybody has a unique configuration of body type, muscle length and specific tightness. Get into a standard stretch such as the hamstring stretch (see page 151) and then slowly introduce an element of sidebending or rotation to feel where resistance and limitation lie.

This is another area where some osteopathic or chiropractic assessment and, possibly, treatment may be appropriate. There may be areas of the spine which are too fixed to allow smooth and free rotation and some mobilization may then enable you to make further progress with your stretching programme.

A caution about becoming overdependent on manipulative adjustments to the spine is worth mentioning. It is not a good idea to use such adjustments on a regular basis as there is a danger of making the joints too mobile. A sportsperson needs stability and strength in the spine and too frequent spinal manipulation may adversely affect stability. It is important to apply manipulative techniques selectively and sparingly as part of an overall approach and not as a panacea. Any sportsperson who is persuaded that they need regular adjustment is probably not getting appropriate treatment. There is no gain in sacrificing strength and stability to hypermobility.

RIGHT-LEFT CO-ORDINATION AND FACILITATION

The brain is divided into right and left hemispheres so that nerve impulses from the right brain supply the muscles and limbs on the left side of the body and vice versa. Most people have developed a 'sidedness' so that they prefer to use one side (usually the right) more than the other. Much potential for increased power and co-ordination lies in facilitating the less preferred side and in balancing the body's tendency to overuse the one and underuse the other.

Top performers have a much greater preponderance of balance in left-right sidedness than the average person. You can improve your own balance by doing exaggerated right-left movements with ordinary callisthenic type exercises. Then try cross-over exercises where you make a marching action on the spot and touch the right knee with the left hand and vice versa. Then, still marching, touch the left heel behind with the right hand and vice versa. This kind of exercise can be incorporated into your warm-up activities so that you bring the less utilized motor side of your brain into operation and enable the favoured side to make a bigger contribution to your total performance.

VISUALIZATION AND BODY USE

You can make considerable progress in changing your body use by creating effective visual images. Images that evoke a fluid or rhythmical style will help your body to reproduce a similar action. Different images may be appropriate for different stages of the competitive situation. I have often found it helpful to visualize the action of a top performer whom I considered to have near perfect mechanics. Sometimes the images may be visions of an animal in flight or more abstract images of water flowing or even words such as 'flow'.

We probably underestimate the inspirational and imaginative aspects of sports performance. It is something like a dramatic production in which the players transcend their normal selves. Again, I have experience of athletes who will play videos of their most admired performers before a major event in order to generate this kind of mental energy. Top performances do require you to step out of the ordinary and become superhuman and to do this you need creative and imaginative inspiration. In the final production the science of preparation joins the artistic flair of performance.

SUMMARY

How to enhance efficiency and energy flow through the body

- Work to achieve a lighter, longer spine.

- Become more aware of how you hold your head and neck.

- Use an experimental, questioning approach to improve how you use your body.

- Use yoga, Alexander technique and martial arts techniques to improve how you use your body.

- Relax the jaw and use breathing effectively to initiate effort.

- Use rotation stretches to release better movement throughout the body.

- Use effective visual images to potentiate better use of the body.

- Use deep massage and mobilization to help start and maintain the process of improvement.

7

GETTING THE BEST FROM YOUR FEET AND FOOTWEAR

Guy Ogden

Most sports people see the foot as an area that requires protection. This perception has been encouraged by sports footwear manufacturers, and a seemingly endless series of modifications to shoe design has resulted. The trend has been towards more cushioning and support. This has further endorsed the view that the foot is a potentially vulnerable area to be encased in as much protective covering as possible.

This view is open to challenge. If you are a top performer you may be looking for perfection, for the extra physical and mental edge that will lift your performance above anything you have previously achieved. A positive training approach to the mechanics of the foot can make a significant contribution to the efficiency of the running or springing action that is the basis of so many sports. In a running action the foot can impart a final spring and leverage which will greatly enhance the efficiency of the gait cycle. If you exercise the foot specifically and choose your footwear carefully you can enhance the mechanics of the foot.

The anatomy of the foot accommodates uneven surfaces. Many of our foot problems arise from the fact that our modern environment has mainly flat surfaces and that we wear shoes from an early age. The result is that our feet get very little muscular stimulation in their use and the intrinsic muscles and ligaments of the foot become weak. Compare the feet of people who walk barefoot on rough ground from birth with city-dwellers who wear shoes from childhood, to see how much straighter and well defined the muscles of the foot are.

THE POTENTIAL OF THE FOOT

The soft tissues of the foot behave in exactly the same way as those in other parts of the body. When they are stretched and released there is a kind of elastic recoil rather like that in a rubber band. This is particularly useful and obvious in the feet of jumpers but it happens to a greater or lesser extent at each footplant in any weight-bearing activity. This elastic recoil is only effective in soft tissues that are well toned. A poorly toned muscle or overstretched tendon or ligament will give very poor elastic recoil. This means that if you want to increase the mechanical efficiency of your foot you will have to exercise it as an integral part of the whole lower limb.

If the foot is not used efficiently more strain will be applied to the hip and lower back region. In a running style where the foot is not sufficiently active in the gait cycle the hip flexor muscles have to work harder to swing the leg forwards. This type of overuse occurs particularly with footwear that has a heel wedge and thick cushioning in the sole. With this type of shoe there is a tendency to land heavily on the heel at each footplant. The cushioning reduces the potential impact and shock but does nothing to promote a more efficient running style. As the foot is insulated from contact with the ground the muscles are not stimulated and tend to become weak.

The problem with making a transition to a more efficient use of the foot is that you may have to undergo some initial discomfort. Changing to a more aggressive use of the foot can involve some barefoot running and an adaptation to shoes with lower heels and less shock-absorbing capacity. You may need to stretch the calf muscles more to accommodate the barefoot training and lower heels.

Many performers use shoes of the type we described as having thick sole cushioning and high heel lifts for training only. They then change to a more flexible, lighter shoe for competitive performances. It would be better to use the same type of shoe for training as for competition. This is because, for optimum performance, you need to exercise the muscles in exactly the way they will be used in a maximal effort. Differences of only millimetres in muscle length can lead to less efficient contraction and to subtle changes of style which may reduce performance. Many track athletes report calf stiffness following the change from trainers to spikes and this is probably due to the sudden alteration in heel height and therefore muscle use.

The extra weight that is a feature of training as opposed to competition shoes is not functional as resistance training because it interferes with style. It is better to devise resistance training that allows you to perform in as close a manner as possible to the way you will use your muscles in competition. Therefore, for running sports, it is better to keep to competition weight shoes but use weighted vests, belts or even weighted gloves or hand weights for running resistance work. This will interfere as little as possible with lower limb mechanics whereas heavy footwear would lead to a very altered use of the hip and lower limb muscles which would not necessarily result in improved performance.

HOW TO STRENGTHEN THE FOOT

To strengthen the foot you need to exercise all the intrinsic muscles that lie deep in the sole of the foot, as well as all the muscles that move the ankle joint.

The best way to do this is to train barefoot on grass or uneven ground and to carry out specific foot exercises as part of your stretching routine. Barefoot training need only be once or twice a week but should ideally be a session where some faster work is done rather than any plodding, steady state work. The idea is to get up on the toes and to use the full leverage available. For running, a light, pattering style should be encouraged which will carry over to running in shoes and prove more effective as injury-prevention than any amount of cushioning in the sole of the shoes. A 'light' style is also beneficial in jumping events and other sports where barefooted training improves foot strength. In addition to pace-work, some springing and bounding on grass or soft ground can also enhance elastic recoil in the foot. Running barefoot on artificial flat surfaces is not a substitute for uneven ground.

The normal foot has a series of arches which are maintained by the ligaments and muscles of the foot. Elastic recoil depends upon the integrity of these arches so that when the ligaments and muscles are stretched in weight bearing they spring back to normal length when the load is removed. A flat foot or one where the muscles are flabby or weak will allow this potential return of energy to be dissipated into the ground. Sometimes there is excessive rigidity in the foot which leads to a loss of accommodation to the ground as the body weight is taken on the limb. In these cases there is a loss of efficiency because the foot cannot deform under a load and return with elastic recoil as the load is removed. A foot that is too rigid may still be moving forwards in the shoe as weight bearing occurs and this can lead to various injury and friction problems. A rigid foot can be improved by osteopathic mobilization and by active stretching. Deep massage to the sole of the foot can soften and stretch the rigid foot and improve its elastic capabilities.

Exercises for the intrinsic muscles of the foot involve as much contraction of the sole of the foot and active use of the toes as possible. Standing on the outside border of the foot and gripping the ground with toes several times until the muscles are tired is an exercise that can be done several times a day. Picking up objects like pencils with the toes helps to activate the muscles so that the foot becomes more responsive. The objective in using exercises of this kind is to potentiate all the movements which the joints are capable of so that the soft tissue network of support to the structure of the foot is strengthened.

The whole issue of foot mechanics is partly a perceptual one. Once you see the whole lower limb as a unit of which the foot is an integral part ending at the toes rather than at the ankle, you can work towards acquiring that extra one or two per cent of efficiency that comes from good foot mechanics.

HOW TO IMPROVE
THE ALIGNMENT OF THE FOOT

A consequence of repetitive weight bearing on flat surfaces is that the muscles and ligaments which support the foot become stretched. In the long-term a condition called hyperpronation may occur where the inside of the mid-foot drops to contact the ground for a substantial part of the weight-bearing phase. A degree of pronation is a normal and necessary phase in the gait cycle but hyperpronation leads to several potential injury problems around the lower leg and may even affect the knee and hip joints. But even where injury does not result there is a substantial loss of efficiency as much of the energy produced for forward movement is lost into the ground when the foot pronates excessively.

Some shoe designs have been produced specifically to combat this problem, with varying success. Unfortunately, the more protective the shoe the less the foot is exercised. The key is to take an aggressive approach to strengthening the foot and stretching the muscles around the hip and front thigh. A lighter, faster tempo in running also helps to correct this problem as it allows less time for the pronation to occur in the stance phase of the gait cycle.

If repetitive injury occurs as a result of hyperpronation and the exercise approach is not effective you may need to deal with the problem by supporting the foot. Sometimes a small piece of chiropody felt fixed along the inside edge of the heel to tilt the heel outwards is sufficient. If this does not work you can try a standard sports orthotic which will support the whole arch on weight bearing. More intractable problems may require the services of a podiatrist who will be able to prescribe a purpose-built sports orthotic to correct your particular foot defects.

——— *SUMMARY* ———
How to get the best from your feet and footwear

- Exercise the foot to improve elastic recoil.

- Use barefoot training to strengthen the feet.

- Choose footwear to balance protection/support characteristics with mechanical efficiency.

- Avoid excessive cushioning, rigidity or heel lifts in footwear.

- Work on correcting foot mechanics and alignment to maximize efficiency.

- Work towards a lighter contact with the ground.

8

COPING WITH SOFT-TISSUE INJURIES AND SPEEDING UP RECOVERY

Guy Ogden

In the process of reaching peak condition most performers experience injury at some stage. The commonest injuries affect soft tissues like muscles and tendons. Although not as serious as injuries to bone, they are, nevertheless, disabling and result in the loss of valuable training time. The chief problems with these kinds of injuries is getting accurate diagnosis of which structures are involved and, more importantly, why the injury has occurred. It is often the case that many top performers repeat the same injury. They frequently get treatment for the local damage but no analysis of the reason for the injury that would enable them to avoid further similar breakdowns.

Soft-tissue injuries may be caused by training errors or mechanical problems. When you get injured it is important to ask, 'Why did this happen?' Was it due to overuse, lack of flexibility, lack of preparation (warm-up), mechanical problems, footwear, diet, mental stress? It may be any one or a combination of these. You need to apply the same questioning attitude to injury that you bring to the whole programme of preparation. An injury is an occasion for potential learning. The more you know about your body's reactions to the stress of training the better. This knowledge will help you to make the decisions that ensure a period of uninterrupted training which leads to peak condition.

Once injured, performers often hand over responsibility to a health care professional. But if you understand the basic principles of repair and rehabilitation you can do a lot to shorten the process of recovery in the periods between treatments. You may be able to start on the remedial stretching of areas whose tightness led to the injury. You may be able to speed up the repair process at the site of damage by using hydrotherapy and some of the natural remedies which are recommended later in this chapter and you might also use positive visualization in healing. You should, if possible, maintain your cardiovascular conditioning by whatever means are available. A lower limb injury need not be exercised. Sometimes non-weight-bearing exercise using stationary bicycles or swimming pools can be used to maintain fitness without stressing injured parts.

Throughout this book we have stated our commitment to natural methods of preparation for top performance. Although this chapter is devoted to ways of speeding up the repair process in injury, there are no short-cuts that do not have long-term damaging consequences. The use of local hydrocortisone injections for inflammation has undeniably dramatic results if accurately applied – but the irrevocable changes that take place in the tissues injected are an unacceptable price to pay. The methods of treatment recommended here are based upon the principle of working with the body's natural healing processes.

AVOIDING THE INJURIES
WHICH ARE DUE TO ERRORS
IN TRAINING

The most common training errors which lead to injury are:

● Continuing to train hard after a competitive performance or maximum effort in training.
● Inadequate warm-up prior to training or competition.
● Too many hard sessions of training set too close together without adequate recovery days.
● A sudden change in training emphasis: for example, a change from steady state to faster training.
● An escalation of training load or a linear increase of load without plateaus of consolidation.
● A sudden change in typical training surface.

These errors are avoidable if you follow the principles of training described in the chapters on muscle physiology and training programmes. A soft-tissue injury should lead you to look at your programme of training and competition to see whether there may be a reason within one or more of the above categories. Every performer is different and what constitutes inadequate recovery for one may be sustainable for another. You need to learn to read your body and be attentive to the signs of overuse. A careful training record helps to identify where things may have gone wrong. For example, you may have increased the training load too much too quickly, or changed from one type of training to another too fast. You may have missed a couple of recovery sessions or done no stretching for a few days.

TAKING CARE
OF A SOFT-TISSUE INJURY

The causes of soft-tissue injury can be reduced to three main factors: changes in muscle chemistry, loss of neuromuscular co-ordination and over-shortening of the muscle length.

After maximum training or competitive efforts there are

alterations in the tissues which leave the muscles very liable to strain or tear for at least 48 hours. If you ignore this and continue to train hard in the days that follow a major effort, an injury is highly likely. Many performers who sustain soft-tissue injuries following such a performance describe how the injury occurred one or two days later during what they describe as a normal workout. During those days the euphoria that follows a good performance may tempt them to train at a rate that is inappropriate.

Inadequate warm-up or sudden switches in training emphasis do not give the muscles enough time to develop the co-ordination required to avoid tear or strain. Muscles under load must contract or lengthen in precise co-ordination if injury is to be avoided. More injuries occur in cold weather because of temperature interference with the rate of nerve conduction, and the effect which that has on overall co-ordination.

Many of the overuse injuries to soft tissues are caused by the excessive shortening that muscles undergo in prolonged periods of training. Shortening will have several consequences. It will interfere with the power of muscular contraction and will affect the overall balance of tension between opposing muscle groups, leading in turn to alteration in the way the body moves. The shortening may also cause tendon problems as the tension leads to undue friction or pulling where the tendons attach the muscles to bones. You may find that the injuries that result from this are located some distance from the muscle contracture that is causing the problem. Unless you deal with the cause you are likely to seek treatment again and again for the same problem.

Tennis elbow is a good example of a condition like this. Tightness in the extensor muscles in the forearm causes a tendon inflammation at a site close to the elbow. Local treatment to that site will have only a temporary effect unless something is done about the excess tension in the forearm muscles. It is possible to give many examples of similar conditions in other sports. If you monitor the tension in muscles on a regular basis and use active stretching schedules as part of the total programme you can usually prevent this kind of common soft-tissue injury.

Once injury has occurred the most important first step is to restrict the possibility of further damage. The first aid steps are often expressed as follows:

- Rest
- Ice
- Compression
- Elevation

These steps, known by the acronym RICE, should be taken as soon as possible. Stop using the affected part as far as possible. Apply cold compresses (not ice directly to the skin). Apply a compression bandage with care to avoid cutting off circulation. Elevate the affected part into a comfortable position.

Strained muscles should repair quickly in fit sportspeople as muscle tissue is well supplied with blood vessels. Extensive tears involving more of the muscle will take longer. Although the problem may have been caused by overtight muscles, do not attempt to stretch the affected ones at this stage. Deep massage is not a good idea as it may cause more damage to vulnerable tissues. So for 24–48 hours keep the treatment to RICE.

After this initial stage you can apply alternate hot and cold compresses and get light massage. When muscle fibres are torn they become weak and, before you do any stretching, you should strengthen them with a series of progressive contractions. When the muscle will tolerate weight-bearing contraction you should start on progressive stretches sustained for up to 1–2 minutes at a time. Deep massage can safely follow this stage.

Once you have reached the deep massage stage, you are ready to begin to apply progressive strengthening to the recovering muscle. The principle is to use the muscle in a 'sparing' way by taking it through the motions with as little stress as possible. A performer with a torn calf muscle might simply patter along hardly lifting the feet from the ground for the first session. Gradually the action can become more pronounced, though at the first sign of major pain you have to go back to a previous stage and consolidate. This technique of rehabilitation is a useful way for performers to manage a return to full training and applies to any injured part.

TOPICAL APPLICATIONS

The use of embrocations and linaments does nothing substantial for a soft-tissue injury other than masking pain by giving a sensation of heat. In fact the names of these products often belie their true nature since they are surface irritants and do not affect the underlying tissues at all. Some performers have found the topical application of witch hazel, comfrey or arnica cream or ointment beneficial. These are natural remedies which should be applied only to areas where the skin is not grazed or broken.

NUTRITIONAL CONSIDERATIONS

During injury there may be advantages in taking a supplement of B and C vitamins. The research in this area is still controversial but there is no doubt that slow wound healing may result from even subclinical deficiencies of these vitamins. A recommended course is a 50 milligram B complex tablet once a day and up to 600 milligrams of vitamin C taken in doses of

200 milligrams three times a day. These supplements should be tapered off as the injury recedes.

A GRADUAL RETURN TO TRAINING

Before you return to any kind of power or speed sessions you should try to exercise the injured muscles by using the longest steady state workout in your programme. Because muscles use only a portion of their available fibres at a time, a long steady workout ensures that all the injured ones will have been exercised. During the course of a session like this you will notice a cycle of dullness in the affected limb as the repairing fibres are brought into use. Provided that you do not experience any sharpness of pain or progressive deterioration following this workout, you can begin to apply graded power and speed sessions.

THE LONG-TERM APPROACH

It is always a psychologically disheartening moment when you sustain injury and see all the careful preparation slip away. At this time it is important to keep a sense of proportion and to take as positive a mental attitude as you can. If you follow the advice in this chapter you can reduce the amount of time you spend sidelined. You can also use the time available to work on other aspects of your preparation, like flexibility. In an enforced lay-off you may be able to break new ground in stretching or strengthening which will improve your performance when you return to full training. Injury may give you valuable time to reflect on your overall approach and to modify your programme if necessary. The mark of a top performer is the determination to overcome setbacks and the willingness to learn from mistakes.

For simple soft-tissue injuries caused by overuse or training errors, we recommend that you seek conservative treatments in the first instance. These are deep massage, hydrotherapy and stretching. In some cases, osteopathic or chiropractic spinal mobilization may be effective. It has been my personal choice not to use electrotherapies of any kind in my practice as I prefer the diagnostic advantages of using the hands and I have treated many conditions that were not helped by ultrasound. However, it has been a popular physiotherapist's treatment for local inflammation and damage, and most sports injury clinics will offer this modality for the type of soft-tissue injuries I have described in this chapter. I have nothing against ultrasound, as long as the cause of the local damage is diagnosed and treated. All these treatments are 'natural' in the sense of not involving 'invasive' techniques like injection or surgery. Some persistent and worsening conditions may eventually need such interventions but these should be a last resort when all the other avenues have been explored.

Performers with injuries are notoriously and understandably impatient to get better. You need to resist the urge to look for quick results and instead to take a longer-term approach and eliminate the cause of the trouble rather than the symptoms alone.

WHERE TO LOOK
FOR THE CAUSE OF THE TROUBLE

The pleasure of watching a top performer in action has to do with the rhythm and relaxed power of physical movement. This perfection of action can only occur when there is complete co-ordination between the muscles involved. Very few performers are blessed with perfect mechanics. When overuse injuries occur, they are often the result of faulty mechanics. You can work towards better mechanics by balancing the strength and the length of your muscles. In this section, three areas of common muscle imbalance and limitation are described.

SPINAL ROTATION

This aspect of human movement is greatly underrated. If your spine will not rotate freely then forward movement is blocked and translated to a side-to-side rocking motion. In ordinary non-sports movements limitations of rotation may be little noticed. At speed or over a period of sustained activity this constitutes a major limitation. You can enhance your range of spinal rotation by carrying out the sidebending and rotation stretches recommended in chapter 13. Occasionally, some limitation of movement in a section of the spine occurs and may lead to overuse injury in muscles around the hip.

You may have restriction of rotation in only one part of the spine or it may be more generalized. Osteopaths, chiropractors, and physiotherapists who specialize in sports injury will be able to assess and help you improve this aspect of your mechanics. If you cannot stand straight and then turn around from the waist up until you can see both your buttocks, then you could benefit from increasing your range of movement. If you increase your ability to rotate freely, then you take off a lot of strain from the hips downward and reduce the likelihood of overuse injury in the leg muscles. For sports where upper body rotation is obviously essential, as in racket sports, there will be obvious advantages in improving range of movement.

To achieve an improvement in spinal rotation you need to overcome the resistance of the tiny postural and rotator muscles that are attached to the spinal vertebrae. You also need to work on the bigger superficial muscles that give profile to the trunk and back and sides of the body. The gains to smooth mechanics from increased spinal rotation can be substantial.

THE HIP AND BUTTOCK MUSCLES

Tension in this group of muscles can be a major cause of injury to the muscles at the back of the leg. Any performer who has had a repetition of strains in hamstring or calf muscles should have these muscles checked for deep contracture that may be causing interference with the sciatic nerve. Deep tension in this group of muscles, the gluteal muscles, is so common that it is worth carrying out routine preventative stretching to avoid the problem. The muscles of this group are powerful extensors and stabilizers of the hip and are used in all lower limb active sports. They are also used extensively in lifting and so, if you are following a programme of weight training, you may unintentionally get over tight gluteal muscles.

The sciatic nerve which supplies the muscles of the back of the leg runs through this area and you can get problems with those muscles if the gluteals are overtight. What happens is that the sciatic nerve becomes irritated and the nerve impulses to the muscles are altered so that the calf muscles may contract at a time when they should be lengthening. The result can be a sudden tear in the muscle on acceleration. A deeper muscle in the same region called piriformis, which is divided by the sciatic nerve, can cause similar problems.

These potential trouble spots can be examined and treated by practitioners skilled in the 'hands-on' treatment of sports injuries, and you can speed the repair process and prevent recurrences by stretching. The 'hands-on' diagnosis is important because often there are no other signs that would give you a clue as to the cause of the problem. In the example of the repetitive calf strain, the cause lies a long way from the site of the injury and local treatment to the calf would not affect the long-term likelihood of further trouble.

THE TRUNK

The trunk is an area of potential weakness. Strength in the abdominal muscles is one of the keys to balanced co-ordination between the upper and lower body. A balance in tone between the abdominal and back muscles also corrects the position of the pelvis which in turn affects the mechanics of the lower limb in action. We recommend that a range of trunk exercises which involve the different groups of abdominals is built into the programme of stretching. The trunk strengthening used in exercise routines by contemporary dancers is particularly good.

Lack of strength in the abdominals may lead to overtight back muscles and eventual back related injuries. In action, a strong trunk enables you to maintain form and style when tired. You can have a highly trained cardiovascular system and powerful limbs and still have weak abdominal muscles. Strong abdominals will support a more lengthened spine. This position enables you to perform with better co-ordination between your upper and lower body. Imbalances should also be noted between pairs of muscles i.e. extensors and contractors. If the quadraceps (front of legs) are highly developed compared with the hamstrings (back of legs), then at maximal effort the weaker partner in the pairing can be overstressed and break down.

——— *SUMMARY* ———

How to cope with soft-tissue injuries and speed up recovery

- Identify the causes of injury so that you can take preventative measures as well as treat the immediate problem.

- Take a positive approach to injury and use the time off full training to improve flexibility and strengthen weak areas.

- Follow the steps of RICE, hydrotherapy, light massage, strengthening, stretching, and rehabilitation exercise.

- Seek advice from sports injury professionals who are trained in 'hands-on' diagnosis.

- Use only natural methods of treatment and explore all the conservative measures possible.

9

HYDROTHERAPY AND MASSAGE

Guy Ogden

Fitness for sports performance is acquired by progressively increasing training loads over a period of time. The problem that top peformers face is how to do this without a breakdown of some kind. If massage and hydrotherapy are properly applied, the recovery time needed between hard sessions can be greatly reduced. In addition, the risk of musculo-skeletal injury is less because the blood and nerve supply to the soft tissues is maintained in an optimum state. These methods of treatment can also greatly assist the performer who faces a series of heats or eliminating rounds preceding the final competition. In these situations it is often difficult to arrive at the final with sufficient physical reserves for the ultimate test.

Hydrotherapy and massage are both natural therapies and therefore may be safely applied routinely over the long term with no adverse effects. Massage has the advantage, not only of speeding up recovery and preventing injury, but also of releasing muscular potential. A regular massage will keep the muscles free from adhesions and partial contractures so that they are capable of more powerful contractions in performance. Muscles that are prepared in this way offer less internal resistance to the direction of effort and allow the performer a smoother and greater range of movement.

Hydrotherapy is the application of water at different temperatures with the aim of evoking a response from the vascular and nervous system. Alternate hot and cold water may be used for increasing blood flow or just cold application for reducing inflammation and assisting coagulation after trauma to soft tissue. The body normally maintains local temperature by dilating surface blood vessels to get rid of unwanted heat or by opening deeper vessels to drive blood to an area that has undergone local cooling. These responses are part of the homeostatic mechanisms of normal physiology. These responses can be used very effectively in the treatment of muscle injury, in speeding up the rate of recovery from training efforts, and in preparing for peak performance. In short, by employing these methods, the performer can 'unlock' the resources of hard sessions which may be bound up by the stiffness and soreness of high performance training.

HYDROTHERAPY:
HOW AND WHEN TO APPLY IT

The physiological effects of hydrotherapy applications are the result of the body's reaction to temperature differences and are not immediately obvious. The short-term application of cold water to a limb has the immediate effect of closing surface blood vessels but also the secondary effect of opening the deeper vessels as the body tries to restore the cooled part to normal body temperature.

This response can be used to great effect in post-exercise treatment to increase blood flow through areas of fatigued and damaged muscle tissue. It has the advantage that the blood flow is increased without the risk of injury that further training might incur. The latest research suggests that post-exercise muscle stiffness is caused by the inflammation that follows micro-trauma to the muscle cells during heavy exercise. If cold water applications are used in the immediate post-exercise period there is a substantial reduction in the amount of stiffness that would normally be experienced following that amount of training. Cold applications help to clear the inflammation caused by the local changes in muscle-chemistry which follow hard exercise.

The effect of heat on a limb follows the same laws of secondary effect. Initially the surface blood vessels open to dissipate the raised surface temperature. The net effect of heating the limb is heat loss to a level often less than at the start. Although the post-exercise hot shower is a favoured habit among many performers, it is not recommended for those who wish to minimize post-exercise stiffness. Stiffness, therefore, has two aspects: first, a degree of actual damage to muscle tissue and, second, sensations of pain that may interfere with smooth action and inhibit further effort on the part of the performer. The correct application of hydrotherapy can minimize muscle stiffness following training sessions and, when it has occurred, can speed up the repair process by natural means. Here is how to do this:

To prevent muscle stiffness: immediately following the training sessions spray or immerse the muscles in the coldest water available, preferably well below body temperature. This is short-term application of cold water lasting two or three minutes. Avoid prolonged immersion in cold water as this may lead to a serious loss of local or body temperature. This short-term local cold application will also slow down the conduction rate of the nerves which register pain and therefore further reduce the post-exercise syndrome.

To speed up recovery between major training or performance efforts: in this case, the application of alternate hot and cold temperatures is used. Apply water from a shower spray or compress to the muscles involved. Start with an application of cold as possible for half a minute and follow with half a minute of an application as hot as possible. The secret is to have as big a contrast as is bearable between the two temperatures. This sequence is then repeated for ten or fifteen minutes. The final application should be a cold one. The process should be carried out twice a day but performers who have problems with stiffness and have a short time-span in which to prepare for further efforts would benefit from more frequent applications. No harm will come from greater use of this method. The effects of the alternating applications are to exert a kind of pump on the vascular system so that there is a rhythmic dilation and contraction of blood vessels and a greatly increased blood flow through the affected area. This helps to ensure sufficient oxygen, nutrition and drainage to the muscle cells and thereby promote healing of damage and a return to normal cell and tissue chemistry.

It should be noted that the application of hot water alone is not recommended. The temptation to soak in a hot bath to ease stiffness should be resisted as the apparent relief lasts only until the body cools down and it contributes nothing to the recovery process as a whole. Embrocations, linaments and other topical applications are also not recommended as they are mainly surface irritants which cause the heat sensors at the skin surface to over-ride the deeper pain sensors which register muscle stiffness. The performer may feel a sensation of deep heat but in fact it is a very superficial heat which does nothing to affect the altered muscle and tissue chemistry that causes stiffness.

To enhance muscle tone and increase blood flow to the muscles: the chapter on the adrenal system described how the effect of adrenalin on the circulation is to provide a greater supply of blood to the working muscles and a reduced blood flow to the surface of the skin. This effect can be further enhanced with a short-term cold application prior to performance. A cold spray of the working muscles before the performer starts warm-up activities will increase local tone and facilitate the neuro-muscular responses. A hot shower or bath on the morning of performance will have the opposite effect and tend to reduce tone and responsiveness of the working muscles.

MASSAGE:
HOW AND WHEN TO APPLY IT

Although there are many different forms of massage which are effective, the form advocated here is the classic Swedish remedial massage which is based upon orthodox western physiology. Swedish massage uses a number of specific movements which have different effects on the soft tissues. Effleurage is a kind of stroking movement but can be applied with great pressure. Petrissage and kneading movements involve deep squeezing and stretching movements. Frictions can be applied across the fibres of the muscles. These main movements are applied specifically according to the state of the muscles as described in this chapter. The benefits of this particular form of massage are well documented and, properly applied, it is one of the most powerful methods of detecting muscular problems, assisting recovery and preparing for optimum performance.

It is not always easy to find good practitioners of Swedish massage as the proper application is strenuous and time consuming but the benefits are well worth the time and effort. Far from being a relaxing luxury, massage should be an essential part of the thorough preparation of the neuro-muscular system of the serious performer.

Many performers are now aware of the benefits of massage in its general application to sportspeople, but there is a need for an understanding of the specific timing and applications of massage in the context of a training and competition programme. The following section describes how and where massage fits into the programme of a top performer.

MASSAGES DURING THE TRAINING PROGRAMME

The aims of massage during the training programme are to enable the performer to undertake progressively harder sessions by assisting recovery, to detect and treat as soon as possible any incipient muscular problems and, if possible, to break new ground by ridding the performer of any old adhesions and contractures in the muscles. This means that the work done on the muscles will be appropriately deep and may itself, in the initial stages, cause a certain amount of post-treatment stiffness. However, the timing of this kind of treatment is critical. It should not be undertaken just before hard sessions of training and certainly not just before a competitive performance.

The rule of recovery described in chapter 4 on training methods applies to deep massage, namely that at least 48 hours should elapse before a session of major effort following deep massage. By deep massage is meant treatment that involves the use of deep fibre or cross-fibre friction or any treatment that leaves the performer feeling stiff or sore. The appropriate type of training to follow such a session would be light recovery. It is very important that, in maximizing muscle efficiency, treatments of deep massage are carried out in the course of a training programme. But it is also important to understand that such treatments may have an effect similar to hard training sessions in that they leave the muscles vulnerable to strain and a period of recovery is needed.

Ideally, the deep work should be done in the early part of the training programme when there is little or no competition. Apart from this kind of deep massage which is directed towards unbinding the muscular potential of a sportsperson, there is a second type of massage which is directed towards enhancing recovery during the training period. This type of massage is less concerned with breaking down the adhesions in muscles and more with enhancing the circulation of the blood and lymphatic systems. To be effective, this type of massage will be deep enough to reach the deeper layers of muscle and would still be unwise the day before or the day of a hard session of training.

As with the advice regarding training sessions, similar attention should be paid to the specific objectives of massage treatment. The performer and the practitioner should both be aware of the position the treatment occupies in the overall training programme. If the performer encounters injury problems in the build-up period, both the training and the massage programme may have to be modified to take account of this.

The programme of training and treatment would be as shown in the chart below:

Day 1   Hard session

Day 2   Light massage

Day 3   Recovery session

Day 4   Deep massage

Day 5   Recovery session

Day 6   Recovery session

Day 7   Hard session
         48 hours recovery period

PRE-PERFORMANCE MASSAGE

The aims of a massage either the day before or just prior to competition are quite specific and different from the training programme massages. Before competitive performance, the massage is designed to increase the responsiveness of the muscles. The movements will be quicker and lighter and less sedating. No really deep work is appropriate at this time as this can run the risk of causing damage to muscle cells that could then become a major muscle injury during the stress of performance. This massage is a 'fine-tuning' treatment.

POST-PERFORMANCE MASSAGE

Muscles in the immediate post-performance period are extremely vulnerable for at least 48 hours. A degree of actual damage to muscle cells occurs during maximum efforts and some slight bleeding and leakage of cell contents affects the surrounding tissues causing the minor inflammation of post-exercise stiffness. Deep massage at this time should not be undertaken until the damage has healed properly. Deep friction work or kneading of the muscles while they are in this state may cause further damage to the muscle fibres and should be avoided. At this time, the appropriate treatment for speedy recovery is light massage and hydrotherapy as described above.

——— *SUMMARY* ———

How to use hydrotherapy and massage effectively

HYDROTHERAPY

- **After training or competition: immediate cold spray or cold shower to the muscles to minimize post-exercise stiffness.**

- **Between training sessions or performances: alternate hot and cold applications. Start with cold and apply half a minute of each temperature for up to ten changes. Finish with cold.**

- **Pre-performance: short, cold application to increase muscle tone and neuro-muscular response.**

- **Avoid the use of prolonged hot showers or baths, especially just after training sessions.**

MASSAGE

- **Deep massage: apply in the build-up period and allow 48 hours before hard sessions of training are resumed.**

- **Recovery massage: apply between training sessions to shorten recovery time and to detect early onset of muscular problems.**

- **Pre-performance massage: apply on the day before or the day of performance.**

- **Avoid deep massage immediately before or after hard sessions or maximum performance.**

10
MUSCLE PHYSIOLOGY

Guy Ogden

Different sports demand differing degrees or combinations of power, speed, endurance, co-ordination or control. In any sport the top performer has to prioritize the major requirement and put the bulk of the training time into acquiring the relevant capability. A fast finish is only really useful if the long-distance performer is up with the leaders at the final bend. However, when it comes to the potential difference between top performers in most sports, we are dealing with fractionally small differences in fitness and ability. The competitive edge may depend precisely on the completeness of your preparation and the attention that you have paid to fine tuning the performer. An understanding of how your muscles react to work can help you to get the best from a training programme and, by maximizing efficiency and avoiding injury, to achieve the competitive edge.

A major factor in bringing the performer to a peak of condition is the extent to which time lost to injury has been avoided. Some performers achieve this for a season of promisingly high performance only to encounter breakdown at the most important final competition towards which their whole season has been directed. This kind of disappointment may be avoided if you have more information about the management of high-intensity training programmes.

The cost to the body of different types of training sessions varies both according to the types of session and to the performer. For example, a skills session may have a relatively low cost at any stage in your programme. An intensive resistance workout will be a high cost session, even to a very fit sportsperson. It is important that you develop a sense of judgement as to how far the training programme is resulting in accumulated fatigue. This kind of self-monitoring is sometimes described as 'listening to one's body'. To act upon this, you may have to depart from a pattern of training that is based more upon administrative or social convenience than upon physiological benefit. It takes a certain strength of mind to withdraw from a session that involves other training partners or which can only take place in facilities that are not always available. But many injuries have resulted from completing workouts that should have been abandoned when the warning signs were there.

Apart from this kind of self-awareness, it is possible to build safeguards into the overall programme so that the dangers of over-training are minimized. The phasing of training, use of hydrotherapy, massage, stretching, sleep and diet all have a part to play in enabling you to make maximum demands on your muscular system. This chapter shows how this can be done.

HOW TO PREPARE MUSCLES FOR MAXIMUM PERFORMANCE

One of the key facts of muscle physiology is that muscles must rehearse the action they are to perform in a manner as close as possible to the action itself if they are to operate with anything like maximum efficiency. The two physiological principles involved are 'recruitment' and 'facilitation' of muscle fibres. We use only a small number of the available fibres in a muscle at low levels of effort. To gain access to the potential of the remaining fibres, so as to enhance the power of the muscular action, the muscle has to be worked progressively towards the level of effort required in performance.

This is a part of the rationale of warming-up. A performer who wishes to be able to sprint at the end of a distance race must therefore include some sprinting in the warm-up activities. If this is done then the fibres that have been recruited in the warm-up activities can be called upon in the performance.

Facilitation refers to the nerve supply to the muscles and the responsiveness of the muscles to demand. To achieve the co-ordination required in a sport, all the muscles involved must respond correctly in terms of lengthening and shortening at the right moment. This requirement implies that the performer should not sacrifice co-ordination and flexibility to power and strength. This idea is developed in chapter 11 on resistance training. The economy of muscular effort is all about maximizing the action of the least number of muscles required to achieve a given performance. Every part of the body that is not directly concerned should be in a state of relaxation. 'Trying hard' may cause a loss of energy. Total involvement may be inefficient as it may well cause tightening of all your muscles. Ski instructors often exhort beginners to relax, and this usually results in an immediate fall. Some muscle groups in skiing need to be under almost constant tension – the 'relaxed' skier is one who can maintain balance on skis with the minimum required tension in the appropriate muscles while relaxing the ones that are not needed. The trick is economy of effort. The energy cost of muscles working inefficiently can amount to that fractional difference between winning and losing.

Many top performers describe how they mentally register tension in different parts of the body when they are in action. They run through a check-list that enables them to make the necessary adjustments to ensure the minimum of internal resistance to their main effort. The seemingly effortless appearance of a top performer in action has to do with this economy of muscular action.

HOW TO PHASE
A TRAINING PROGRAMME

Fashions in training methods change over time. There is more than one way to achieve the peak of condition that top performers seek. As stated in the previous section, sports make a combination of specific muscular demands for which the training programme should provide. The outcome of a protracted tennis final may hinge on stamina rather than the edge on skill or speed. A cross-country ski race may hang on hill-climbing power where stamina is evenly matched.

In the past, the tradition in training programmes was to separate the components of a fully prepared performer into phases of training largely dictated by season and weather considerations. The current state of knowledge about muscles implies that it is difficult and potentially risky to switch demands in training abruptly. A more physiological approach combines all the components of the programme throughout the season so that the transitions in emphasis are more gradual.

There are differences in the length of time it takes to acquire muscular capabilities and in the length of time they can be expected to remain without further training inputs. For example, it is well known that endurance capabilities take longer to acquire than speed or strength. It is also true that, once acquired, stamina lasts longer than speed without further training. An exclusive emphasis on one type of training for too long can lead to a loss of capability in other areas. A long period of stamina work may result in decreased flexibility and a loss of the ability to change pace. A training programme based mainly on high quality speed work may lead to a gradual loss of stamina during the season.

If there are several muscular capabilities to be covered by the training programme then decisions must be made about the priorities and phasing. All performers will need to do this whether they are experienced sportspeople with capabilities acquired from years of participation, or whether they are new-comers or young sportspeople.

My preparation for the European Veterans 10 Kilometre Road Title was designed to enable me to inject changes of pace during the course of the race. To acquire this ability I used a kind of inverted pyramid session of interval training where the long efforts were placed at the start and end of the session and the short efforts in the middle. My session would look like this: 4 mins, (2 mins recovery), 3 mins, (2 mins), 2 mins, (2 mins), 1 min, (1 min), 1 min, (1 min), 2 mins, (2 mins), 3 mins, (2 mins), 4 mins. This is the reverse of the usual practice of pyramid training where the short efforts are done at the begin-ning and end of the session. My method gave me the ability to inject a change of pace during the race. The session gave me a total period of cardiovascular demand that closely resembled a 10 kilometre race. In the Championship I employed efforts of increased pace from the middle of the race. In the event this strategy worked well and the leading pack diminished as the pace wound up. A final surge with a kilometre to go was enough to secure the title.

In principle, skills training where necessary can be carried out throughout the programme as it presents few risks. It is essential that, in sports where hand-eye co-ordination or reac-tion time is important, these skills are maintained throughout the entire programme. The neuro-muscular co-ordination needed must be facilitated in daily workouts and cannot be called upon suddenly if it has not been rehearsed.

In sports where endurance, speed and power are needed it used to be the practice to build what is termed 'base', by carrying out endurance training first, followed by power work and finally the speed component was added. The problem with separating these phases is that the muscles find the transition difficult and some risk of injury occurs. Here is an outline of three phases of a programme where the emphasis shifts from endurance through power work to speed work:

Phase 1   Endurance priority:

E   E   R   E   R   P   R   R   E   R   S   R   R   E   R   E

Phase 2   Power priority:

P   R   R   S   R   R   E   R   P   R   R   S   R   R   P

Phase 3   Speed priority:

S   R   R   E   R   P   R   R   S   R   R   E   R   S   R

E=Endurance   P=Power   R=Recovery   S=Speed

The endurance sessions are followed by only one day of recovery training as they are less likely to render the muscles liable to injury. Out of the same total of 15 training sessions, the endurance phase allows five sessions of endurance work, whereas in the power and speed phases there are only three sessions of power and speed work as these require two recovery sessions to follow.

This scheme is an example of a way to ensure that the three qualities of endurance, speed and power are maintained while particular emphasis is being laid on one quality for a limited period.

It may make sense for sports where this combination of qualities is required to reverse the traditional method of endurance base followed by speed. There may be advantages to the performer in achieving an improved style or form from the exaggerated action of faster work and then extending this gradually in longer, sustained work. This reversal of the normal practice may be suitable for both experienced performers and newcomers for different reasons. In the case of the experienced performer, who already has a good background of endurance work, the way forward will be to carry out the sustained work at a faster pace. The newcomer will bring a more efficient style to the sustained work and build upon that rather than upon the poorer style that often goes with slower training.

HOW TO ORGANIZE
A PROGRAMME TO MINIMIZE
MUSCLE FATIGUE

The importance of adequate recovery is emphasized throughout this book. On a week to week basis the performer who follows this advice will be inserting regular recovery sessions into the normal cycle of training. But also emphasized is the importance of increasing training loads progressively in the quest for new peaks of fitness. Performers who increase training loads in a linear fashion are likely to encounter accumulating fatigue to a point where an injury or illness is imminent. An alternative method which allows both a progressive increase in training load and intensity and yet allows for adequate recovery is the 'plateau' method.

The plateau method very simply involves a linear increase in training load for a limited period which is followed by a block of recovery training or a temporary return to the training load at the start of the increase. Some performers find that a cycle of increase over four weeks with a return to the load of week one on the fifth week is a good formula for avoiding overload. In this way progression is achieved with consolidation. Other performers use a 'hard-week easy-week' pattern to achieve a similar result.

We do not often think about sleep unless we are having trouble getting it – but the physiological repair processes that occur during sleep are essential to the performer who is making maximum demands on the body. High intensity training programmes of the kind that top performers now require mean that more sleep is needed. The top performer should take an additional sleep during the day. This advice is easier for the full-time sportsperson than for those who must fit their training into work and domestic schedules. A performer who manages to take only one hour of extra sleep per day will be getting the equivalent of one whole night of extra sleep per week. This may make a major difference to the accumulated fatigue levels of a high performance training programme.

The chapter on massage and hydrotherapy describes the contributions these methods can make to recovery time. If a recovery system is built into the training programme and, if extra sleep, massage and hydrotherapy are used, it should be possible to push the training demands to new limits. Natural aids like these have no long-term ill-effects and only enhance condition.

How to read the body

The signs of over-training and accumulating fatigue are familiar to most top performers. The temptation to do just that one extra session or effort in order to gain a supposed advantage over rival competitors is familiar to everyone who has been involved in top performance. Often it is just that extra effort that throws away a season's careful preparation. The important thing is not just to recognize the signs of over-training but to act on them. Even where an important event is a short time away there are ways of minimizing the effects of over-training. Here are the signs to watch for:

- resting heart rate ten beats or more above normal for the performer
- weight loss, loss of appetite
- difficulty in sleeping, waking tired
- persistent muscle soreness
- frequent low grade infections
- loss of interest in training, staleness
- difficulty in completing hard sessions

Any of these signs should lead the performer to review the training programme and seek a health check. Blood tests will reveal the presence of infection or anaemia and these tests should be carried out if a recovery period fails to affect the symptoms.

Mental fatigue or staleness often precedes a physical injury and is a sign to take seriously. A drastic tapering of training may be enough to cure the problem but long-term persistent fatigue of this kind may mean that hormonal and blood chemistry is altered and a more protracted period of rest is needed.

Mental flexibility is one of the key qualities that a top performer should cultivate. A slavish commitment to schedules of training when the body is giving signs of stress is a mistake that can cost dearly. A performer who is slightly under-trained but mentally fresh and enthusiastic for competition will almost certainly out-perform the one who has peaked and is mentally stale. Typically, it requires more strength of mind to back off training than it takes to push the body through another hard session.

HOW TO TAPER
BEFORE A PERFORMANCE

Most performers use some method of tapering training before competitive appearances in order to build up physical and mental resources. Opinions as to how much tapering is required vary widely. A major factor in achieving a peak will be your willingness to refrain from further efforts in attempts to 'round-off' training or because of fears of losing condition.

The amount of tapering must be related to the different physical and mental demands of different sports. The training demands of endurance events probably require the longest tapering. The experience of many performers who have returned from an enforced lay-off to produce world-class performances suggests that there may be as yet unidentified changes in blood chemistry after prolonged periods of training. These may take up to three weeks or a month to restore to optimum levels. If this is so then tapering hard training for less than a fortnight before major events may be insufficient. Soviet research demonstrated that for explosive events, such as weight lifting, no 'take out' sessions should be completed in the final ten days before a major competition.

We suggest that performers experiment with different lengths of tapering, bearing in mind that it is designed to restore mental as well as physical resources.

HOW TO USE DIET
AS AN AID TO RECOVERY

The immediate post-training needs are for fluid replacement. The best kind of replacement fluids are water and dilute fruit juices. Where fluid losses are high the potassium and magnesium contained in fruit juices are a valuable aid to restoring the body's tissue chemistry to normal. Tea and coffee have diuretic effects which make them unsuitable as replacement fluids and should be avoided at least until the basic fluid requirements have been met.

In the immediate post-performance period the diet should consist mainly of fresh fruits, raw salads, vegetables, potatoes, bread and cereals like rice. These foods make the least demands on the digestive system and provide most of the nutrients that are lost in prolonged exercise.

——— *SUMMARY* ———

*How to apply the physiology
of muscle to training programmes
for top performance*

- **Train all the abilities required throughout the entire programme of preparation: emphasis may be greater on one aspect rather than another at specific stages of training.**

- **Read the body:**
  1 Increased heart rate, weight loss, persistent muscle soreness, poor sleep and frequent infections are signs of over-training.

  2 Abandon individual training sessions or planned competitive appearances if necessary.

  3 Mental fatigue or 'staleness' is a sign to take seriously as it often precedes a physical injury.

  4 Insert more recovery days, if required, especially after key hard sessions or competitions.

- **Taper training before performances: do not underesti-**

mate the amount of tapering required. Experiment with different lengths of tapering. Use only recovery or skills sessions in the tapering period.

• Prepare muscles for maximum efforts by rehearsing briefly during the warm-up period. The full range of efforts that will be required in the event ensures that all the appropriate muscle groups have been facilitated and recruited.

• Use diet as an aid to recovery:
1   Replace fluid as soon as possible using drinks which are rich in potassium and magnesium such as fresh fruit juices.

2   Avoid diuretic fluids like tea and coffee.

3   Increase fresh vegetables, fruit and cereal consumption and cut out dairy foods and red meats in the immediate post-performance period.

CHAPTER

11

EXERCISE
AGAINST
RESISTANCE

Guy Ogden

Resistance training is a method of training where you make the action more difficult than it would normally be. The training effect of this kind of work gives you more power and strength and local muscle endurance. You can achieve the right degree of increased difficulty in a variety of ways depending on the power/strength needs of your sport. For runners, repetitions of hill running or sand dune training would be a simple way to carry out resistance training. Weight training is a favoured form of resistance training for several sports and can be organized as circuit training to cover a variety of exercises to strengthen different parts of the body.

Many sportspeople use some form of resistance training to increase local muscle strength, power and endurance. In power based events the benefits of this kind of training are well recognized. You may sacrifice some flexibility in the process of building strength through weight training but there is no doubt that some performers have made major breakthroughs in a season following extensive resistance work.

As with planning training programmes in general you have to make a judgement about the aims of a resistance programme which relates to the specific requirements of your sport and to your own strengths and weaknesses. Your weight-training schedule must therefore be as specific as any other part of your training programme.

There are advantages in carrying out the work in a circuit training form with a series of exercises designed to build strength in the postural and auxiliary muscle groups. The key factor in weight training for performance is that the exercise must be as close as possible to the action of the muscle in your sport. An extension of the knee, with your foot stationary on the floor, is not the same muscular action as takes place when your body is in motion and the weight of your body is moving over your foot. Some authorities also claim that the muscle contraction should be carried out at the same speed as required in the sport. This means that you need to look very carefully at weight training programmes to evaluate how far they are appropriate for you. It is better to tailor a schedule specially for yourself than to follow a generalized routine with a training group.

The danger is that you can lose flexibility in two ways. First, by the loss of length in muscles that goes with increased tone and, second, because exercising a group of muscles always involves changes in the length and tension of other muscle groups. You can avoid these problems by carrying out stretching and flexibility work as described in chapters 8, 10 and 13. If you steadily increase the weight load lifted you will sacrifice speed and flexibility. Lighter weights, exercised faster for a longer period, will result in better local muscle endurance and this is the favoured regime for most sports outside weight lifting itself.

To get the greatest benefit from weight training your schedule should entail a progression which enables you to reach a predetermined maximum somewhere about two-thirds of the way through your season. You can then progressively reduce the weight lifted and increase the speed and number of repetitions so that the slowing and binding effects of weight training are minimized and speed and endurance are maximized.

The need to approximate as closely as possible the muscular co-ordination and action of your sport would appear to favour free weights over fixed machines of the multi-gym or Nautilus kind. The advantage of free weights is that the auxiliary and postural muscles of the body are exercised in their supportive role when you are lifting. When you use a weights machine you are often isolating a muscle group while the rest of your body is supported in a way that is not typical of the body in motion. Many performers will claim that they have benefited from the use of fixed weights. We are looking here at ways in which a top performer can maximize the benefits of resistance work and introduce some refinements in the way this type of training fits into an overall programme.

HOW TO PLAN
MORE EFFECTIVE RESISTANCE
WORK

To many sportspeople resistance work means simply weight workouts in a gym. There are many alternatives to this which can be just as effective in enhancing potential. We have already mentioned the advantages that are gained from resistance work that makes minimal interference with the co-ordination of movement. This is not a new idea: dancers have used ankle weights, sprinters have harnessed themselves to car tyres, middle-distance runners have worn weighted belts or vests, boxers have sparred with heavy gloves. In these examples there is minimal interference with the way the muscles are normally used except that they all have to work harder.

This kind of resistance training will have a local effect on the main active muscle groups and also be of benefit to your heart and lungs. It may be desirable to use free weights or fixed-weight machines to build extra strength in particular areas with some performers – but, once this remedial work has been done, the type of resistance work chosen should have speed and flexibility in mind. The transition from the ability to train with heavier weights to enhanced performance in your sport is the acid test of resistance work.

The increase in muscle power has to be functional and available. You could easily create a resistance programme that interfered with your normal muscle action. Running with weighted boots or with a heavy rucksack is a kind of resistance session but interferes with running action in a way that leads to a distortion of natural style and will lead to no marked improvement in performance.

The most effective way to use the active type of resistance work is where you pronounce or exaggerate your action. Avoid using resistance in a plodding, steady state or recovery type of session as this may lead to defects in your style and form. The resistance session is a high intensity, hard session which will need recovery days to follow. Remember always that the effectiveness of your resistance training has to be measured by improvements in your performance in competition and not by progress in the resistance workouts. It is possible to become better at lifting weights with no actual improvement in performance.

In my preparation for the Veterans National Cross Country Championships in 1984 I considered that the race would be won by whoever was strongest on the hills and I planned my programme of training to ensure that I had that quality. I used small hand weights weighing up to a total of three pounds in each hand in sessions of hill repetitions lasting up to two minutes. This meant that I was working against a resistance of nearly half a stone with minimal interference to my running action. The chief contender, Taff Davies, was an outstanding veteran who had won the Championship for the past five years, and was faster than me on level ground. In the race I pushed hard on each hill and was able to put sufficient distance between us to ensure that his faster finish was to no avail.

PUTTING
A RESISTANCE WORK SCHEDULE
INTO A TRAINING PROGRAMME

To maximize the benefits of resistance work you need to position it to optimum advantage in the overall programme. The best way to begin is to sit down with your coach or advisors and decide what aims you have for this part of your programme. If there are weak areas in your style these can be assessed and some objectives set down. These will form the basis for deciding the content of your resistance work schedule. You then need to decide on the progression and phasing of the work to be done. This needs to be tied into the training phases and the plans for competition.

Throughout this book we have emphasized the need for methodical and systematic planning in training programmes. We believe that performers should have a questioning approach to all the aspects of their programme and be able to account for the reasons for doing things one way rather than another. This develops a sense of personal responsibility and independence in the performer and affords some protection from manipulation or thoughtless adherence to habit.

Below is an example of how a resistance schedule could be positioned in the context of an overall programme of training.

EARLY SEASON	EARLY-MID SEASON	MID SEASON
remedial weights (specific weak areas)	circuit training	active resistance training

——— *SUMMARY* ———

How to use
weight training effectively

- Use weights exercises which replicate the muscle action of your sport as closely as possible.

- Use a parallel schedule of stretching to avoid loss of flexibility.

- Explore the use of resistance work that makes minimal interference with the muscular action of your sport.

- Phase the resistance work towards lighter, faster work as the competitive season approaches.

- Plan a resistance work schedule that is specific to your sport and to your specific requirements.

- Carry out no more than two sessions of resistance work per week. Leave at least two days of recovery between workouts.

- Avoid building bulk in muscle groups that are not directly involved in your sport.

- Use circuit training with light, free weights to achieve basic conditioning in all the muscle groups essential in your sport.

12

TRAINING
PROGRAMMES

Guy Ogden

Fashions in training methods change. Looking at how top performers have trained over the years we can see that there is more than one way to achieve sporting excellence. But fitness is acquired by the same physiological process whatever the training method used. It is essentially the body responding and adapting to stress. This is what is meant by the term, 'training effect'. If you understand this you can see why the crucial equation in exercise physiology is the relation between stress and recovery. We find that many top performers are more concerned with the stress part of the equation than with recovery. They want to know more about the intensity and quality of workouts than about the recovery needed to make them effective.

Training has to be progressive. Once having acquired a level of fitness, you do not get any fitter unless you increase the intensity or volume of workouts. You need to break new ground in training sessions to surpass previous personal records. So, in this chapter, we look at ways to enable you to train harder – but, unless recovery is adequate, you will not be able to sustain the harder workouts and you will also get less training effect from them. The apparent paradox is that, while we emphasize rest and recovery, we expect that you will actually train harder following our guidelines. The workouts will get harder but the space between them will get longer.

What is a
Hard Session of Training?

You will be able to describe what it feels like to carry out a hard training session and probably be able to give an example of such a session in your particular sport. The subjective feelings of effort and fatigue experienced in such a session are not only related to time, speed and distance but to what state you were in when you started the session. What you normally find easy can be very difficult in the days that follow a maximum effort or when you are trying to get fit after illness or injury.

Exercise physiology shows that to achieve a training effect from a workout you need to raise your heart rate above a certain level. For trained sportspeople in their twenties the threshold would be around 145 beats per minute or 70 per cent of their maximum heart rate. If you train at a rate much less than this you need to carry out a huge volume of training to get any results. Some endurance sportspeople favour steady state training where a high volume of work is carried out at a relatively easy pace and this kind of conditioning is often referred to as 'base' work. It gradually leads to loss of excess weight and more efficient oxygen utilization. But, once a background of this type of training has been carried out, any further improvement will be very slow. We have found that heart rates of around 120 beats per minute are typical of experienced endurance athletes carrying out a steady state, long-distance session. This level of effort will lead to very little change in performance.

We find that the training schedules of many performers blur the distinction between hard and easy sessions. Too many of the workouts are carried out at a rate of work that is too high for recovery but below what would be an appropriate stress session if the performer were adequately rested. For well trained individuals, the training threshold of around 145 beats per minute is too high for recovery but not enough to create the stress needed to obtain a significant training effect.

We suggest that if you label the workouts as either stress or recovery then a heart rate of no more than 120 beats per minute for the recovery sessions is appropriate. If you are fit a workout at this rate will feel comfortable and not require any mental concentration. The purpose of this recovery workout is to give your body time to make adaptive responses to the previous stress session. The point of continuing to train in a recovery period is that you maintain neuro-muscular co-ordination and facilitation and keep the muscles supplied with circulation more effectively than if you rested completely.

Top performers will need to take their heart rates to levels well above the training threshold during the stress sessions. On occasions they will need to take it up to and beyond 90 per cent of their maximum. There are many workout combinations of effort and recovery available which can be used to achieve this objective. Interval and repetition workouts, resistance training and varied pace endurance workouts are well known to top performers. A hard session in heart rate terms is one where you bring your heart rate up to 80–90 per cent of maximum several times during the workout. This is the principle that underlies interval-type training and has a major training effect on the cardiovascular system. To get the greatest benefit from this kind of workout you should have at least two days recovery after it. Effort that raises the heart rate above 180 beats per minute several times in a workout will lead to fatigue factors that require at least 48 hours recovery. Heart rates during competitive performances in some endurance sports may hover around 85 per cent of maximum for the duration of the event. It makes no sense physiologically to apply any other than the lightest of workouts following such an output.

——— ENSURING THAT ———
YOUR TRAINING PROGRAMME
IS COMPREHENSIVE

Top performance in sport depends upon a range of physical and mental capabilities. A characteristic of top performers is that they are meticulous and thorough in their planning and preparation. Initially, you need to analyse the qualities you will require to be successful and then you need to provide for these in the way you put together the training programme.

One of the key qualities may be mental flexibility. Some performers are easily discouraged by unpredicted changes in temperature, food or organization. You need to be able at least to ignore such changes and at best to turn them to positive advantage. Mental flexibility before or during an event will allow you to adapt your performance tactics to the unfolding situation rather than fall victim to other performers' competitive decisions.

This kind of adaptability to circumstances over which you have no control is the mark of a top performer. To acquire it, you need a combination of mental and physical training. It is no use having the mental flexibility to react to a sudden change of pace if you have not carried out the necessary physical training. Some of this preparation is simply thorough homework on the conditions and competitors you are likely to encounter.

In my preparation for the San Diego Veterans World Championships I made the mistake of not finding out enough about the course for the 10 kilometres which turned out to be perfectly flat and fast and well suited to track-trained runners. The hill sessions I was still doing less than a month before the race were not relevant. In the race I was unable to answer a sudden tactical change of pace early in the race by the top American veteran Barry Brown and had to settle for the silver medal although the race was won in a time I had been well capable of earlier in the year.

During the course of a competitive season there may be different requirements at different stages. National championships may take place in very different circumstances to Olympic finals and the training programme should take account of this. The formula that worked well for the performer at mid-season competition may be inadequate when confronting world-class opposition.

You need to guard against settling into a training programme and doing workouts that are convenient and that you enjoy doing but which may be inappropriate preparation for your season's targets. The programme must be relevant.

——— *SUMMARY* ———

*How to train more effectively
to enhance performance and
avoid injury*

- Make your training programme progressive: better performances come from more intensive training.

- Organize the training to maximize your ability to carry out hard sessions by planning adequate recovery periods.

- Check your heart rate to monitor the effectiveness of your training sessions.

- Ensure that the programme covers all the qualities required for the long-term goals.

- Be aware of the specific purpose of each training session and of each stage in the overall programme.

- Be flexible in your willingness to adjust the programme to avoid excess fatigue or injury.

- Set medium-term targets to test the effectiveness of your programme.

- Spend time on planning a programme, commit the plan to paper and keep a training record.

13

STRETCHING:
AN INTEGRATED
APPROACH

Alan Evans

Earlier chapters have emphasized the improvements to performance brought about by the right mental attitude, by training for power, speed and endurance, and by the crucial role of recovery in the whole process. While there is a significant corpus of knowledge about the training aspect, much less is known about recovery. There is also little knowledge about the role of development of flexibility and suppleness. Flexibility is not an optional extra, but a vital component of preparation for top level performance in all sport. Stretching, which increases flexibility and suppleness, acts as an organizing and binding agent that gives a new dimension to training for speed, power and endurance. Suppleness and flexibility are essential components of high levels of fitness. Those who aspire to quality performance, paticularly over any length of time, neglect stretching to the almost certain detriment of their optimum level of performance.

Suppleness is the source of the human being's elasticity; it is, as John Jerome emphasizes, 'the spring loading in the biomechanics of athletics'. The soft tissue of the body reacts dramatically to overuse, underuse or inappropriate use, and such activity leads to injury and deterioration in health and wellbeing. When men and women in the economically richer nations led much more physically active working and domestic lives the need for stretching exercises for building strength and suppleness on the muscular skeletal system was less significant; in contemporary society it has become essential, not just for competitive sport but for general health.

A PERSPECTIVE ON STRETCHING AND STRENGHTENING

We recommend a standard stretch which involves moving in a relaxed fashion into a gentle stretch of about ten to thirty seconds until a modest degree of tension builds up. As this tension begins to abate move a fraction into what Bob Anderson calls the 'developmental part' of the stretch and hold for ten to thirty seconds. Under no circumstances should you bounce into a stretch or move beyond the first hint of pain. At the slightest suggestion of pain adjust the position of the stretch or eliminate it for the time being from the programme. Stretching is a qualitative activity with highly individualistic persona; it is essential therefore that each stretch feels right for you and only you can judge that.

The standard stretch will meet the needs of most performers, although someone returning to fitness after injury might include a 'tighten-relax' stretch approach if this approach feels comfortable and appropriate in the circumstances. The debate on whether to warm up before stretching, stretch before warming-up or to interweave the two has generated more heat than light. If, for instance, you are going on an early morning training run, it is unwise to begin stretching as soon as you get out of bed as the body needs to loosen up and the body temperature and metabolism need to be raised. Always wait a minimum of fifteen minutes before you begin a stretching routine.

Light running, if necessary on the spot, for one to five minutes is a good way of warming up the body before commencing a stretching programme. It is difficult to set an ideal time limit for such a warm-up: it should be as short as is necessary for the performer to know that the body is ready to begin stretching. It is also worth noting that stretching itself contributes to the warm-up by lifting the temperature of soft tissue and also helping to increase the metabolic rate. Stretching integrated into a warm-up session helps to reduce the resistance of the muscle fibres and soft tissues to joint movements, thus preparing the body for a more efficient, injury-free training session.

The nature of the training activity should determine the character and content of the warm-up stretches. For instance, if the activity is mainly running, the stretches should relate to the key areas of the calves, quadriceps, hamstrings, hip flexors and lower back. This is also the case for post-activity stretching.

It is essential both in the warm-up and warm-down that you should stretch those muscles that would be stressed and strengthened by the activity in the training session. The warm-down session requires a substantially longer time. The harder and more intensive the training session the longer and more thorough the stretching programme will need to be.

CAUTIONS AND BENEFITS

Stretching is a benign and easily controllable activity and the limited number of dangers can be easily and readily understood. These are summarized below:

● Do not bounce into a stretch until after the muscle has been stretched and only then if you are about to embark on explosive movements like jumping or sprint starts.
● Do not stretch to the point of pain.

- Do not stretch cold or directly injured muscles or connective tissue.
- Do not stretch your more supple side first.
- Do not stretch your thighs before your calves.
- Do not stretch your hamstrings before your quadriceps.
- Do not stretch muscles that are in various forms of contraction from the adrenal system.
- Do not leave antagonistic muscles weak and unstretched.

The benefits far outweigh risk for the performer.
Stretching:

- improves performance
- reduces the risk and incidence of injury
- speeds up recovery after a hard training session
- returns the body to balance after the stress of highly concentrated specialist training
- develops the capacity to 'listen' to the body with greater awareness
- assists in the process of warming-up and warming-down the muscles and other soft-tissue areas affected by the stretch
- improves posture
- releases tension

IMPROVED PERFORMANCE

The evidence which suggests that stretching can increase flexibility around a joint and thus improve co-ordination and ease of movement, resulting in more economical use of energy, has grown in the last ten years. Stretching lubricates the muscles, helps to eliminate or reduce stiffness (and hence resistance in muscle fibres) and produces supple and resilient connective tissue.

Increased flexibility and elasticity in the soft tissues of the body in turn ensures that energy released is used with maximum economy for improved performance. A bicycle which has not been oiled for two years is a perfectly safe and efficient vehicle for use on the roads (particularly compared to the standard motor vehicle which is only about 22 to 24 per cent efficient) but the amount of energy needed to propel it will be far greater than if the bicycle were well-lubricated. Similarly with the human body: the lubricant is an activity-related stretching and strengthening programme. This is referred to as the 'oil-can effect'.

LIMITING
AND REDUCING INJURY

It has been argued, in earlier chapters, that a judicious blend of stress and recovery sessions will lead to an improvement in quality of performance and that the frequency, timing and even the mental process of the recovery sessions are as crucial to the improvement as are the stress sessions themselves. This is certainly true for stretching. We advocate systematic, comprehensive and regular stretching before and after training, sometimes augmented after particularly hard training sessions by a further period of stretching before retiring to bed. Sebastian Coe, at his peak in 1979, was the holder of three world records on an incredibly low weekly mileage base for a top athlete. It is significant that his training programme included a high proportion of quality work interwoven with a stretching routine reputed to be between one and one-and-a-half hours daily! Serious performers in all sports should stretch for one hour several days each week.

Stretching is one of the few activities where there is 'gain without pain'; it has no negative by-products. Stretching facilitates three physiological processes. First, it realigns the muscle fibres that have been disarranged by shortening and stressing in those parts of the body that have borne the brunt of the activity, thus helping to lengthen the muscles and assist recuperation of the connective tissues. Second, it enhances the flow of oxygenated blood which is rich in nutrients, and expels the chemical detritus of hard physical effort. And, third, it reinvigorates and recharges the neurological networks of the muscular and connective tissue systems and gives the body tone and balance. There is little doubt that quality stretching can reduce, or almost eliminate, stiffness or soreness after hard training sessions and thus prevent an injury occurring a few days later in a rather mundane and low-key training session.

Particular sportspeople and particular sections of the work force are prone to specific injuries and ailments. For instance, soccer players, especially in the United Kingdom, tend to be stiff in the legs; indeed, although they are trained athletes, many of them have less flexibility in the legs than non-athletes, and frequent groin injuries are the bane of their sporting lives. Office workers, as a group, have short hamstrings, and a high proportion of them, not surprisingly, suffer from pain in their lower backs. Regular and thoughtfully-focused stretching could greatly reduce the injuries of soccer players and improve the general health of office workers.

SPECIFICITY, BALANCE AND INJURY

In an effort to improve strength and achievement in competitive sport, the emphasis on highly specialized specific training regimes is both inevitable and inexorable. Such an approach, however, places great strain and stress – to the point of overuse – on particular muscles, connective tissues and other soft-tissue areas of the body. It has, for instance, been demonstrated that strength training reduces flexibility by between 5 and 13 per cent for a period of up to two days. The more specific and specialized is the training of particular performers, the more important it becomes to build into the training programme a medley of stretching and strengthening exercises to bring the body back into balance. As a by-product this may well improve performance and will certainly inhibit or eliminate the danger of injury from overuse and over-specialization.

The need to devote more time and priority to stretching and strengthening muscles and the counteracting muscles (the antagonists) is clearly demonstrated by the frequent common injuries that plague substantial numbers of players in those sports such as soccer, rugby, hockey, running and cycling.

I had direct experience of coping with the problems of over-specialization in the training for a major endurance event when, in 1980, I took a party of 14-16 year old students to cycle across America in 38 days, covering an average of more than 100 miles per day, with only one rest day. The tour was planned on the notional basis of alternative hard days (e.g. 150 miles) with easy days (e.g. 70 miles). In the pre-tour training substantial time was devoted to overall fitness and flexibility, through intensive circuit training and other quality training approaches. In the actual training, regular daily speed work figured larger than lengthy endurance runs. I am convinced that it was the combination of the overall fitness and flexibility training and the 'stress-recovery' approach which enabled the youngsters to succeed on the Trans-American Expedition. The pre-tour training mileage of 2000 miles would not of itself have got us across America.

STRETCHING, ANATOMY AND POSTURE

Throughout this book we have stressed the need for performers to increase the awareness of their bodies and to develop a capacity to listen to their bodies. Stretching provides a particularly valuable listening board, providing the raw data and analytical tools to monitor recovery and stress, and to integrate the lessons and insights into modified training programmes and into the actual performance of the chosen sport.

Many practitioners in sport at all levels have postures which are inefficient and cause energy to be devoted to sustaining their bodies' inappropriate bio-mechanical positions. There are, in other parts of this book, references to and suggestions for the need to take corrective action. It is important that the performer takes on the challenge of retaining or acquiring good posture while being duly sensitive to genetic constraints. Postural deficiencies cannot be tackled safely by traditional linear stretches but rather by combining specific strengthening exercises with linear and rotational stretches, and then monitoring carefully the improvement in posture and its significance for improved performance in the individual's particular sporting activity.

In the chapter on body use the central issue is the spine and the need to lengthen it. The complexity of human movement is further explored by considering the action of the shoulder and pelvic girdles and their encapsulation by the soft tissues of the body. As a species, homo sapiens, in advanced technological societies, is prone to weak stomach muscles, stiff necks and tightness at the back of the shoulders. Most of us have, at some stage, suffered from bad backs; significant numbers in the population have short hamstrings and the frustrations which they bring in their train. The lack of mobility in the hip joint is also a source of great concern. Tension caused by life style, stress and lack of appropriate physical exercise conspires to make the problem bigger and more intractable. But, in fact, the situation is not without hope. Time invested in stretching and remedial exercise can significantly improve posture and performance.

TRAINING AFTER INJURY

Stretching, massage and hydrotherapy all have important parts to play in reducing the period of enforced lay-off of the injured performer. It is not possible to begin stretching if you experience any pain in the injured area. It may well be possible to stretch and strengthen the antagonistic muscle groups, thus preparing for the time when it would be possible to stretch the soft tissue which experienced the injury.

In some cases the *soft-tissue* manifestation of injury is some distance away from the actual joint, connective tissue or muscle fibres which sustained the injury; for example, lower back pain may arise from stiffness or hamstring injury. In these circumstances it is often possible to treat the cause at an early stage and then accelerate remedial stretching and other treatment of the apparent area of the injury.

——— *SUMMARY* ———

Stretching and strengthening for improved performance

- Go into this activity gradually to keep risk of injury to a minimum.

- 'Listen' to your body.

- Warming down is as important as warming up.

- Flexibility, ability to relax and posture are all improved.

- Incorporate stretching into your training routine to acquire economy of effort and reduced risk of injury in performances.

- Do not stretch painful, injured areas.

14
A GUIDE
TO
GENERIC STRETCHES

Alan Evans

The stretches set out in this final chapter are by no means exhaustive. There are several books (listed in the bibliography), the subject matter, photographs and diagrams of which refer solely to stretching, while a small number consider the issue of stretching and strengthening in considerable depth and sophistication. There are, however, few books which capture all the essential elements that are necessary to understand, analyse and evaluate stretching as an essential component along with speed, strength, endurance, co-ordination and precision in striving for sporting excellence.

The illustrations which follow show what can be described as generic stretches, as they cover the main soft-tissue areas of the body that require stretching. Particular programmes required by performers could draw on this basic list of stretches and augment it from one or more of the basic texts.

It is worth repeating that we are strongly committed to rotational as well as to linear stretching, and to converting and modifying second and third stretches into rotational form from traditional linear stretches. From our reading and discussion with sportsmen and women, with individual medics and para-medics with an interest in sports medicine and athletic performance, with practitioners of alternative medicine, and from our own direct experience, we are convinced that stretching which is successfully structured, organized and applied can have a profound and lasting effect on performance in sport and in body maintenance.

It should be noted that apart from stiffness from heavy exercise, individuals create muscle tightness. As a direct result of our reactions to everyday stresses or threats, real or imagined, we hold tension. In this way we gradually lose our natural childhood flexibility. Becoming aware of your reactions to daily stress could allow you to let tension go; for example, notice whether you are holding your shoulders and neck tense while driving or talking with your boss. If there is tension, drop your shoulders, take a deep breath and let it out slowly. Your body will relax if that is your intention and the focus of your attention.

NOTE: In the following illustrations, the specific areas of pressure generated in each stretch are shown by means of cross-shading.

SOLEUS AND ACHILLES STRETCH

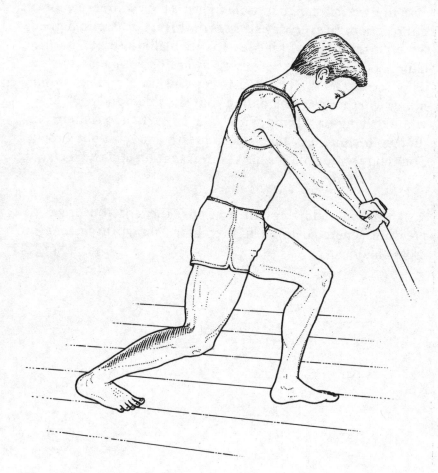

- Toes forward.
- Take all your weight on the rear foot and press the knee towards the floor.
- The stretch is felt deep and low in the calf.

GASTROCNEMIUS STRETCH

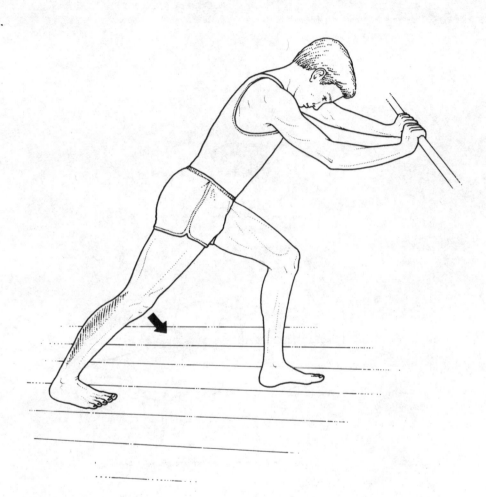

- Toes forward.
- Rear knee straight.
- Lean forward to feel a stretch at the upper part of the calf and behind the knee.

QUAD AND FRONT HIP
STRETCH

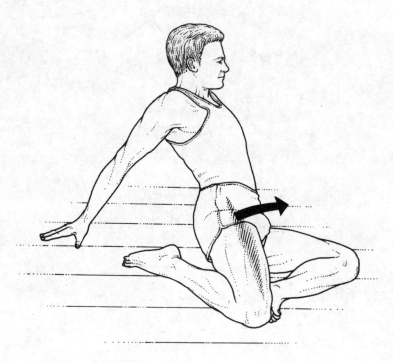

- Push the hip up and forward to feel a stretch in the upper thigh.

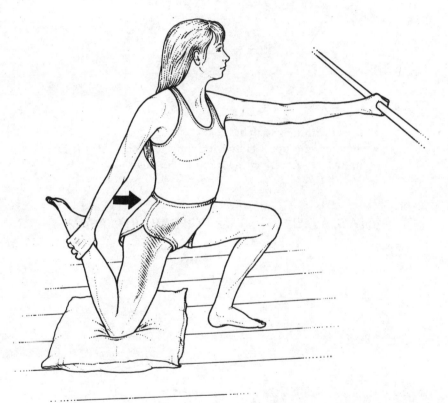

- Kneel on a cushion and hold onto a bar or chair.
- Hold the kneeling ankle at arm's length and push the hip
  forward to feel a pull in the upper/outer thigh.

QUAD STRETCH 2

- Kneel with toes straight back.
- Support your upper body with your hands and lift the hips up to feel a stretch at the front of the thigh.

HAMSTRING STRETCH WITH TOWEL

- Keep the back straight and head up.
- Lean forward from the hip.

HAMSTRING STRETCH

- Legs apart.
- Keep the back as straight as possible.
- Head up.
- Move into the stretch from the hip not the mid-back.
  Progression: From the full stretch start to turn the upper
  body to the front to feel a stretch at the side as well.

GROIN STRETCH

- Soles together.
- Stretch by arching the lower back and pushing the hips
  forward.
- Do not strain with the arms.

HIP, GLUTEUS AND
LOWER BACK STRETCH

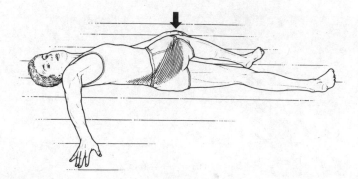

- Lie on your back.
- Bring one knee over and press it down with the opposite hand.
- Turn your head away from the knee.
- Relax the body to let the back rotate.

GLUTEUS AND THIGH STRETCH

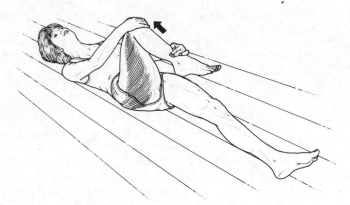

- Lie flat.
- Bend the knee and pull the lower leg towards the opposite shoulder with one hand on the knee and one on the ankle.
- Relax the head and neck during this stretch.

DEEP HIP BENDING
STRETCH

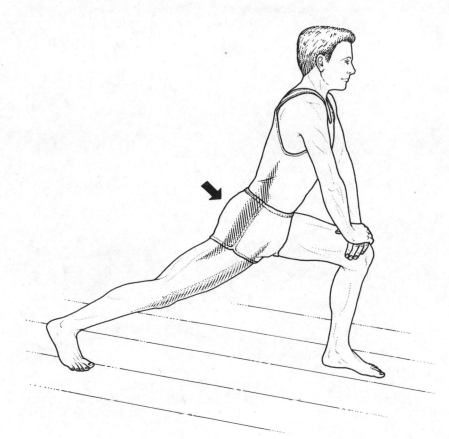

- Take a controlled long step forward and lower gently to stretch the front of the hip of the rear leg.
  Progression: Hold onto a bar and rotate away from the rear leg to feel the fascia stretch across the hip and up the side of the upper body.

GLUTEAL STRETCH

- Side sit on the outside of the bent leg.
- Keep your back straight and head up.
- Bend forward over the knee from the hip to feel a stretch in the gluteal muscles.

PLOUGH

- Lie flat on the floor and tuck the chin well into the chest.
- Bring the legs up and over the head. There is no need to touch the floor with the feet at first. The legs can be bent at the knees but gradually straighten them.
- Relax and feel the stretch at the back of the neck and between the shoulders.
  Progression: Straighten the legs slowly to feel a stretch along the back and behind the legs down to the ankle.

TRICEPS AND SIDE BEND
STRETCH

- Feet apart.
- Bend knees slightly.
- Pull elbow across the back of the head and side bend slowly at the same time.

PECTORAL STRETCH

- Hold bars or a door frame at chest height.
- Lean into the stretch and then bend the knees slightly.

THE F-TEST

How do you rate as a complete performer? You can use the F-Test as part of a programme of self-assessment.

The F-Test is intended to help you assess progress in five key areas:

> Focus
> Fitness
> Fatigue
> Food
> Flexibility

It is recommended that you run through the Test at periodic intervals, perhaps every six months. You simply construct a grid based upon the questions given below and a rating chart of 0–10. The score of 0 would mean very poor and the score of 10 would indicate excellent.

Ratings of 7 or less for individual parts of the Test would mean that more time needs to be spent on those particular aspects of the overall programme. Top performers should be looking for scores of 9 and 10 throughout the Test.

FOCUS

1 I have medium- and long-term goals.

2 I am enthusiastic and feel highly motivated to achieve my goals.

3 I am completely committed to my goals.

4 I am not easily distracted from my goals.

FITNESS

1 I have a planned, progressive programme of training.

2 I am carrying out training sessions that are relevant to my competitive goals.

3 My programme distinguishes between stress and recovery sessions.

4 I use resistance work appropriately.

FATIGUE

1 I use rehabilitation methods such as relaxation techniques, massage and hydrotherapy on a regular basis.

2 I monitor and revise my training programmes using a checklist of over-training symptoms.

3 I incorporate an off-season for recovery.

4 I minimize stress in other areas of my life.

FOOD

1 I eat regular, well-balanced meals and take plenty of fluids.

2 I avoid junk foods and caffeine-containing drinks.

3 I eat plenty of fresh fruit, salads and wholegrain cereals.

4 I take balanced formulae of vitamin and mineral supplements and avoid food fads.

FLEXIBILITY

1 I set aside a regular time for stretching each day.

2 I spend time on warm-up and cool-down activities each session.

3 I monitor stiffness following stressful workouts and spend extra time on flexibility work in the recovery days.

4 I balance lower limb, trunk and upper limb flexibility.

BIBLIOGRAPHY

Alter, J. *Stretch and Strengthening*. Houghton Mifflin and Co., 1986.

Anderson, R. *Stretching*. Shelter Publications Inc., 1980.

Astrand, P.O. and Rodahl, K. *Textbook of Work Physiology*. McGraw Hill, 1977.

Balaskas, A. and Stirk, J. *Soft Exercise, The Complete Book of Stretching*. Unwin Paperbacks, 1983.

Bergh, U. *Physiology of Cross-Country Ski Racing*. Human Kinetics Publishers Inc., 1982.

Bernhardt, D.B. (ed.). *Sports Physical Therapy*. Prima Publishing and Communications, 1988.

Connolly, C. and Syer, J. *Sporting Body, Sporting Mind*. Cambridge University Press, 1984.

Francis, L. and P. *If It Hurts Don't Do It*. Prima Publishing and Communications, 1988.

Galloway, J. *Galloway's Book on Running*. Shelter Publications, 1984.

Gallwey, T. *The Inner Game of Tennis*. Cape, 1975.

Hlavac, H. *The Foot Book*. World Publications, 1977.

Hutchinson, M. *The Book of Floating*. William Morrow & Co., 1984.

Jerome, J. *Staying Supple*. Bantam Books, 1987.

MacLeod, D., Maughan, R., Nimmo, M., Reilly, T. and Williams, C. (eds.). *Benefits, Limits and Adaptations*. E. and F.N. Spon, 1987.

Miller, B. *Sports Psychology and Running*. Reed Books Pty., 1987.

Solverborn, S. *The Book about Stretching*. Japan Publications Inc., 1985.

Wirhed, R. *Athletic Activity and the Anatomy of Motion*. Wolf Medical, 1984.

Wootton, S. *Nutrition for Sport*. Simon & Schuster, 1989.